PUT YOUR ARMS AROUND THE CITY

PUT YOUR ARMS AROUND THE CITY

James W. Angell

Fleming H. Revell Company
Old Tappan, New Jersey

A man's mother is so tissued and woven into his life and brain that he can no more describe her than describe the air and sunlight that bless his days.

CHRISTOPHER MORLEY

Contents

O LORD, who fearlessly set Thy face to go to Jerusalem, we are afraid of our city. We recoil from its stone shoulders, its acrid, smoky breath, its raucous noise, its garish lights, its dark doorways and shadowy figures. It is ugly and alien, and we want to flee.

O Lord who, when seeing Jerusalem, loved it enough to weep over it, may we see with open eyes our own city—its beauty in the clean edge of fresh-cut steel, in the marvelous shapes of molded plastic, in the powerful grace of mighty machines. And may we see with Thine eyes the people of the streets—their faces, some etched with wear from inhuman loads of hardship and privation, some masking fear and hate, and revealing our common humanity of tragedy and hope. Then may we be drawn to our city by admiration and compassion, for it desperately needs people with eyes that see and hearts that care, and who are not afraid. Amen.

MAYNARD D. SMITH

Acknowledgments

MY SPECIAL THANKS to Helen Douglas whose affectionate persistence and many hours at the typewriter turned the manuscript from a vague dream into a fact; to Morgan Harris for his professional eye and ear, his pleas for simplification of expression and rejection of my original chapter titles; to the members of the Westwood Presbyterian Church congregation for sharing the exciting task of trying to rearticulate the faith for persons relatively new to the urban situation; and to my own beautiful family who are constantly putting their arms around me.

Introduction

FOR PERSONS who have always lived in large cities the problems of an urban existence may not loom so large, but many of us are new here. We came from the small towns of Iowa and the farms of Texas. We came from communities where everyone in town knew who got the top awards at high-school graduation, and where most families owned just one automobile. We moved from Mississippi to Chicago because a brother-in-law had said it was better here. We left Dawson Springs in favor of Tampa because a new university was opening and there were no heating bills in the wintertime. We wanted in on the action, the fun, the dough. We found it, just as they said.

We found loneliness, too, and we went whole days without hearing our name pronounced once. We forgot there were seasons of the year because we were busy trying to survive. We were too tired on weekends to go to church. We had more money, but less love. We had no desire to return from where we came, but the city was often too much for us. As though something good inside us had disappeared, or died.

America is now an overwhelmingly urban nation, and an increasingly secular one. What this book attempts to do is to answer the question—what does a relevant belief in God have to do with living in cities like Los Angeles or Detroit? Is faith part of an abandoned small-town past? Or, keyed into an urban style, does it still have power to fill emptiness and to exalt persons above everything else? To lead all sorts of men toward more significant and satisfying life together?

Faith and the city are made for each other. Both share in the dynamic shifts of a revolutionary time. Some would turn Christianity into a form of nostalgia. More would ask for its rethinking and recasting in terms of man's new spirit. Greer Garson said the other day, "I like to keep my horizons wide and my waistline narrow." This effort is based upon the belief that there are new horizons of possibility both for the City and the Church, and that, enthusiastically claimed, they will help explain and fulfill each other.

JAMES W. ANGELL

I
LOVE IS A METROPOLITAN THING

1

Beauty Rides the Bus

The final mission of the city is to further man's conscious participation in the cosmic and historic process. Through its own complex and enduring structure, the city vastly augments man's ability to interpret these processes and take an active and formative part in them, so that every phase of the drama it stages shall have, to the highest degree possible, the illumination of consciousness, the stamp of purpose, the color of love.

LEWIS MUMFORD

THIS IS THE CITY.

Los Angeles, California, a spatter-paint, galaxy-sized community on the southwest coast of America's most populous and fastest growing state. A city dedicated to fun and the future—an exhilarating mixture of sun, science, sin and the cinema. Color it black, white, yellow, brown and red.

I live here. I carry a Book.

While Los Angeles is different, every city is different, and every city is the same.

This is about city people, city problems and the life of faith.

It calls men to love the city with passion and imagination, a vocation guaranteed to produce beautiful people wherever they live.

Beautiful people are the ones who have made it big in theatre, letters, politics, or the stock exchange. Yesterday, they were in Palm Springs. Tonight, they'll emerge from a coal-black limousine in front of the Beverly Hilton, and tomorrow fly to Aspen. They are the people with flair who tell us which cigarettes taste best and who show us how to live with style, even if we're stuck with a factory job, a boring law practice, or responsibility for getting meals for a husband and five children.

There are other beautiful people in the city, too, people who have learned to rejoice, both in the world as it is, and in a world they are trying to bring to birth. They are the poor as well as the affluent, the neglected as well as the noted. They are found working in restaurants and printshops, candy factories and hospital laundries. They live in plain houses or basement apartments. They ride the buses. People are beautiful whenever they are committed to live for others.

The prayer to ". . . let the beauty of the Lord our God be upon us" (Psalm 90:17) is a prayer all can make.

Beauty is many things. It is shrimp boats sleeping in the harbor. It is sunlight, hitting the top row of windows of the Occidental Center at seven in the morning. It is black-violet mountains as the sun plunges into the sea. It is snow on evergreen branches, the smell of grease in a bicycle shop. It is a silver plane with someone you love on board, touching down at International Airport, rolling through the darkness toward the terminal. It is jacaranda blossoms floated from graceful branches into the middle of the street, off-to-school kisses, books with writing in the margins, a little lake of faces on the first day of a Head Start class, or long-whiskered Mr. Pierson at a retirement home, looking like a prophet and saying with forgivable pride, "Oh, me? I was a miner's miner!" It's the public library, a Sunday school piano.

Most often it is people—people who, for a few seconds, are lifted out of themselves.

Barney sells flowers near the entrance to the Security Bank. Crippled by palsy, his spirit is, nevertheless, healthy and gay. He's a merchant. One afternoon, I decided to buy a bunch of carnations from him.

"How much are they?" I asked.

"A dollar and a half a dozen," he answered. "Can I wrap up a dozen?"

"Mostly the pink with two or three of the red. "

I produced two one-dollar bills. When he didn't have the right change, I attempted to pass off the difference as a tip. A tiny accusation of patronage in his gentle gray eyes told me I had made a small but serious mistake. We got correct change at a coffee shop. As he twisted his way down the street, his salt-and-pepper hair blown crazily by the ocean wind, I decided he was surer of his humanity than I was of mine.

Marie is eighty-two. Every day she alights from a Wilshire bus and walks into a large veteran's hospital nearby to serve as a volunteer. With her crispy hat tilted at a jaunty angle, she forms a gay vignette as she moves arthritically about the dance floor to "Josephine," while elderly men patients queue up for their turn to dance with her.

Cities today are turning black, and the discovery by the black man that he himself is beautiful is a greater plus for our age than the transplanted heart. Dr. Martin Luther King helped to pull the curtain on that truth. He left us a poignant parable concerning the part the black struggle has played in chiseling new forms of beauty. King and his wife were visiting in India. He remembered their standing on the beach at Cape Comorin where India ends in a glorious tip of sand. It was twilight.

As the waves unfolded in almost rhythmic succession and crashed against the base of the rock on which we were seated, an oceanic music brought sweetness to the ear. To the west we saw the magnificent sun, a great cosmic ball of fire, appear to sink into the very ocean itself. Just as it was almost lost from sight, Mrs. King touched me and said, "Look, Martin, isn't that beautiful!" I looked around and saw the moon, another ball of scintillating beauty. As the sun appeared to be sinking into the ocean, the moon appeared to be rising from the ocean. When the sun finally passed completely beyond sight, darkness engulfed the earth, but in the east the radiant light of the rising moon shone supreme. To my wife I said, "This is an analogy of what often happens in life." We often have experiences when the light of day vanishes, leaving us in some dark and desolate midnight—moments when our highest hopes are turned into shambles of despair, and we feel that there is not another light. But we may be consoled that God has two lights, a light to guide us in the brightness of the day when hopes are fulfilled and circumstances are favorable, and a light to guide us in the darkness of the midnight when we are thwarted and slumbering giants of gloom and hopelessness rise in our souls.

Beauty thus starts from within, culminating in the belief that there is a place for me in life which will leave emptiness if unfilled. When we accept ourselves because God has accepted us, we become free to live out our relief and gratitude among others. This is the battle that must be won by man in the city if he is to find his true existence.

A useful key to beautiful living is represented by Jesus of Nazareth, who is best understood today as the "Man for others." In Him, men and women still continue to discover the life that is most meaningful and free. This is the side of His nature that grabs modern men. Speculation concerning His divinity is meaningless. Looking to Him for help on what it means to be a man, what it takes to achieve a reasonable life together in the city, or what in life warrants a total commitment of self, brings Him on stage as never before.

Jesus no longer comes to us from outer space, but from inside the heart of history. He qualifies as history's redeemer by being part of it. The orthodox view presented God as working from outside—from a detached realm—breaking through a barrier separating eternity and time. He came to earth, pierced the mortal situation and, by the perfection of His obedience, accomplished deliverance for all who put their faith in Him; but an increasing number of people do not subscribe to a compartmented interpretation that has earth in one compartment, God in another.

The beauty of the Galilean, by the older interpretation, is the beauty of One who comes as a messenger from out there. In newer theologies His beauty is the beauty of One who exposes the claim of God from within. The idea of God parked out in space is ridiculous to modern man. God as an immanent Lord, who enables man to conquer his own fear and frustration, he understands.

Another part of the beauty secret has to do with weakness, with the cross. When anything is perfectly executed we shout, "Beautiful! Beautiful!"; yet, we too, are often more beautiful in failure than in success. We wanted to do everything correctly, to be controlled and neatly self-sufficient. Then things all went to hell. The house collapsed, and we stood there in dirty, helpless ashes. Suddenly we were beautiful.

The Lord of life is no celestial hero who rushes onto the scene, knocking out the world's eyes with magic tricks. He is, rather, the Servant with the weary face and punctured hands, trudging the dark streets of East Los Angeles. He is the place where two streams of life run together and give up their separate identities. He is the Man man wants to be, with the love of God pressing subway-hard against our humanity, liberating us for hopeful life in the world.

Christianity sees beauty in a child born in a barn, and in a Man dying on a hill. It sees beauty in things as they are, and as a moral upheaval more far-reaching than the world has ever seen before. It sees the beauty of the city man has made, and beauty in the process by which the city is remaking man into an original-by-God.

Today storm warnings are not only up; but the flags are being ripped by wind and hail. These are also days of optimism, for they mean that old infections are being brought out into the healing air. Storm warnings announce that tough and exciting questions are being asked, and that terrible, frightening circumstances are calling forth a fresh loveliness from a life being lighted by star shells. One America has died. A new one is crying and kicking its way into our affections. It remains a time of beauty.

In the days of Arthur, a knight once rode forth in search of the grail, the cup from which Jesus was supposed to have drunk at the Last Supper. As Launfal's horse's feet rattled the bridge on his way out of the castle that morning, at the beginning of his noble mission, he tossed a coin to a beggar by the side of the road. Many years later, the mission having failed, Launfal returned, broke and broken by failure. He was on foot now, and the ownership of the castle had passed from his hands.

Dressed in ragged peasant clothes, he encountered, near the gate through which he had once sallied forth with pride and confidence, the same poor fellow. As he shared his final crust with the man, and they drank from a common, partly rusted cup, the grail miraculously appeared.

Life often seems lacking in brilliance. We see society point first to these persons, then to others, naming them "the beautiful people." They have been noticed lunching at Century Plaza or arriving, dashingly dressed, at the Philharmonic tea. Meanwhile, others plod along unnoticed; but the prayer of Psalm 90 is for all. It is not a prayer to admire the beauty of others, but to become beautiful ourselves.

With the model God has provided in the Carpenter, in a world as much in need of repair and hope as ours is, the chances for winning an Atlantic City ribbon look rather good.

2

Getting Your Arms Around Seven Million People

The web of love relationships has been broken and it is time for compassion . . . the Church must take the World into its arms while still continuing to fight it.

C. KILMER MYERS

THE WAGONS are still rolling west. From covered wagons to station wagons, California has been the land of gold and the golden land. Since 1940 it has become to America what America was to the immigrant populations of Europe in the late nineteenth century. Southern California alone now has seven million people.

Though it is possible to meet someone who was born in Los Angeles, the person who sells you underwear in the May Company, or the twenty-four-year-old who passes you on the freeway in his maroon vw with snow skis fastened vertically, is more than likely, from Joplin, Missouri, or Loup City, Nebraska.

Some are disappointed and return home. A car with Oklahoma license plates, headed east, had a sign scotch-taped on the rear KEEP YOUR DAMMED GERANIUMS. WE'RE GOING BACK!

22

Most stay and try to build houses of happiness for themselves in a city which, in area, is the largest in the world, exceeding even New Jersey in square miles. Before the year 2000, metropolitan Los Angeles is expected to stretch from San Diego to Santa Barbara, a community more than 300 miles long.

Russell Baker has described it in its present state as

. . . a large body of automobiles surrounded by road signs . . . bordered on the top by sunshine, in the middle by smog, and on the bottom by little old ladies in tennis shoes . . . a city famous for sun glasses, Humphrey Bogart, saffron slacks, Chinatown, and blonds of odd proportion.

By night, Los Angeles is a sparkling bracelet worn on the wrist of the Santa Monica mountains. By day, it can appear grim beyond description . . . a palm-bordered junkyard of rusted dreams, mystery cults, crowded convalariums, and life as shallow as the name of one of its star attractions, the Pink Pussy Cat.

Other cities, too, have their distinctions. Places like Boston, New York, Philadelphia, Washington, and St. Louis long have been members of the urban Hall of Fame. But now Seattle and Minneapolis typify human centers where the issues of metropolitan living are full blown also, as mayors and commissioners agonize over how to keep up with the need for enough houses and jobs, schools and stoplights, parks and air terminals.

Today, most of America lives in the city with its vulgarity and violence, its beauty and loneliness. A question many city residents, especially the newly arrived, try to answer is this, Is it possible to love persons in the large impersonality of the city? Is there a way to get your arms around millions of people?

At times, it seems impossible. Though we travel a thousand miles an hour and the world has become a village, people within cities are famished for community. A member of the Hundred Thousand Mile Club said, facetiously, "Traveling is great these days—your breakfast in Dallas, your lunch in Paris, your dinner in Cairo, and your luggage in Rio!" However, for all this coming and going, satellite communications, instant news, and one-worldness, we remain a lonely crowd, pressed together in a high-speed elevator watching the floors of years click by, yet strangers in the night.

High-rise dwellers relate through the smallest morsels of information. The man above is known only by the fact that he is heard to snort each night around dinnertime, "I'm not going to work for that jerk one more day!"

One day after I had put my trash cans on the street for the weekly pickup, I found a note from a man who lives nearby, saying I had set my can too close to his property. I was sad because I knew this was all we had found it possible to say to each other, after living for more than a year as neighbors.

There are, though, bright exceptions. One day, I was working at home alone with an ax. It slipped and severely injured my hand. I was not able to drive my car to the hospital. I ran to the house of a nextdoor neighbor, but no one was home there. The hand was bleeding profusely and I was beginning to feel desperate. Suddenly, I noticed a dry cleaning truck coming up the street. Seeing trouble, the driver braked to a stop. Not only did he transport me to the hospital, he waited outside the emergency room for two hours until he was assured that I was all right and that my family had been informed. Three cheers for the city!

In the Westwood section of Los Angeles, a father, mother and five children were leaving for the South Pacific, where the father was to assume an important assignment with the Peace Corps. Word spread that the Hartsocks were moving, whereupon the neighbors got together and had a party in the middle of the street. They got permission from the Department of Public Safety to block off the avenue for three hours on a Sunday afternoon. When the hour came, out they went into the street, laughing and milling around as if it were the Gooseberry County fair. They decorated their houses, drank lemonade and made funny little speeches and said loudly and clearly, "We acknowledge being bound together in the bundle of these parcels of adoining real estate, no man is an island, and a part of us is leaving with this family."

Community in the city is not ordinarily geographical. It is psychological, cultural, crisis-centered. People are drawn together not by abutting yards but by shared values, computer dates, or bumper stickers. One reads, P.S. I LOVE YOU; another pleads for support for a bond issue, a political candidate, or the saving of Rustic Glen from the clutches of a land developer.

The most important success factor in city living is the attitude a person takes toward others, with whom he shares the city's variety and delights, its problems and its pain. Enter love. Love understood as a controlling principle of behavior rather than as an emotion which says, "I can't help the way I am." Though Christians are not the only people who love, they are taught love as something a man does, as well as something he feels, perhaps even in place of what he feels.

In the brief months of his ministry, Jesus met all kinds—old and young, scholars and beggars, sick and strong—and had compassion for each. Cities like Denver and New Orleans, Tulsa and Tacoma are also holy lands where all orders of men pass by. They are, by turn, playgrounds and prisons, classrooms and crime centers, theatres and tenderloins. While one has to be selective to survive at all, all men are entitled to dignity and understanding. The limiting factor in urban life is not usually circumstances, but a reluctance to love those who are different, or those we simply don't like.

Frederick Speakman explains the familiar dilemma.

We may never have said it to ourselves in so many words, but most of us, somewhere along the road, have said something like this: "Love of all mankind is church talk which never comes to grips with people as they really are. My hat's off to anyone who can make any kind of go of it. But my heart is made— and remember I didn't make it—my heart came equipped with a certain stubborn earthy stuff that simply can't go round emoting over the many unloveworthy people I know, so there's no point in pretending that I can. That crude lout down at the office who so deliberately needles my nerves, or that smooth liar who took me in so completely yesterday, or that crass, strutting big wheel who barged into our neighborhood . . . by what magic am I supposed to feel anything but resentment, distrust, and a justified desire to have nothing to do with such as these?"

25

Then he answers his question.

> *But what if Christian love was never meant to begin in the way we feel toward people?* What if Christian wisdom dismisses as quite obvious the kindergarten fact that of course you and I will always be fond of some people, and not at all fond of others? What if Christ never expected you and me to sit around trying to force, trying to manufacture affectionate feelings toward people who consistently dig and rub us the wrong way? Wouldn't that refocus the picture?

From the Los Angeleno's point of view, the dialogue, rewritten, might read as follows:

> There are all these freaky people around here. The UCLA student I passed on Broxton with long hair down his back, his books in a burlap bag, the topless-for-lunch places, the all-night movies, the miserable hotels. There are the Bel Air mansions with picture-book lawns and electrified gates. People jammed in courtrooms are waiting for their cases to be called, others are standing blank-faced in long lines waiting to discuss welfare applications. Six thousand meet in a city park to hear an appeal for Black Power, while others call in reservations for the Candlelight Ball, or seek excitement at Santa Anita. A bowling alley is crowded with customers at 4 A.M. Freeways are never still. The city is too big, too stratified, too engineered, too rich, too poor, too busy to be talking about love—love between persons.
>
> What if, instead of this odd-shaped, crazy-dyed, hostile, avant-garde array of human beings passing daily before our eyes, we saw individual men and women, each trying with boots or bicycle, cause, skill, or new divorce decree to find his place in the scheme of things? What if, looking upon these new-frontiers men, we recognized those in whom God has made a unique investment, and for whom He has a specific purpose? What if we imagined God was hoping He might communicate His concern through *our* concern—wouldn't that refocus the picture?

26

This is starting to get our arms around other people. It is the first step in the process of taking other people seriously whether they live in Cincinnati or Portland.

The Christian faith helps equip people to live in the city by increasing their capacity to love, without needing to be loved in return. It produces love that can love without waiting to be asked, and love that can love that which is different from itself. Because of its unilateral character, it cleverly disarms the enemy. It cannot be threatened or destroyed by racial myths, changes in neighborhoods, pressure of numbers, or signs that say KEEP YOUR DAMN NOSE OUT OF MY BUSINESS. Rather than presenting urban man with threats against which he is under pressure to protect himself, the city, by its kaleidoscopic variety becomes the place where love finds new freedom, new width. The Christian is at home wherever one man needs, or asks for, the hand of another. To him, the sirens along the boulevard are not noisy distractions, but caring sounds that mean help is on the way!

In the final shake-out, it is this for which men really hope. Only skin-to-skin, life-to-life encounters can redeem the city from anonymous death and enable men to penetrate a bloodless wall of switches, punch cards, and rules for behaving in mass society.

The Christian faith was brought up in the city. Bethlehem was small, but Jerusalem and Rome were large and powerful centers of urban life even in Biblical times. Other than the Sermon on the Mount, the most memorable address of the New Testament is the one Paul delivered in metropolitan Athens. Corinth had the same problems Kansas City has. Antioch was the Milwaukee of the Mediterranean. Faith knows the city well and what it has to say about love, persons, ethical obligation, the stranger and the marketplace is still relevant.

Faith also improves man's possibilities in the city by encouraging him to make the dilemmas of his total environment his own.

Ross Greek, who spends most of his time working as a youth minister on Los Angeles' Sunset Strip, spoke to a gathering of church women on a Thursday morning. He said part of the answer to trouble there lay in having parents take greater responsibility and in knowing where their children were during the late hours. Following his talk, a woman came to the speaker's stand, and, after customary pleasantries, remarked, "This is not our problem. Our young people of Roseland Park know how to entertain themselves without going to the Strip."

Sunday at 2 A.M., Ross's telephone rang. It was the same woman's voice on the other end. Through tears, she stammered out a request, "My daughter was one of several teen-agers arrested last night in a riot on the Strip. Will you meet us at the jail, and see what you can do to help?"

The health of all America's cities—Knoxville or Chicago, Toledo or Fort Worth—depends upon the willingness of people to accept the city's total life as part of their responsibility and to become involved with it. The suffering of one is the peril of all. That is the lesson many communities have learned since the angry, smoky summer of 1965.

When people we care about are knocked down by adversity, we go where they are. We put our arms around their shoulders to transfuse hope. We look into their faces and remind them of our confidence in them. Today, our cities need this kind of embrace. To become serious about loving people, even by the millions, is to help snatch them from the fire. In the process, something dramatic and good may happen to the way we feel about ourselves.

3

Will the Church Learn to Dig the Urban Style?

In almost direct proportion to the increasing importance of the city in American culture has been the withdrawal, both physical and spiritual, of the Protestant Church. If Protestantism gives up the city, it virtually gives up America. Yet that is precisely what it has been doing.

TRUMAN DOUGLASS

I SAW A HOUSE on Hilgard Avenue painted in red, blue and yellow stripes and came home raving about it.

"You'll never believe this," I told the family at dinner.

The next day, I promised the children we would drive by and let them see it.

As I slowed our Datsun for a close inspection of the bizarre sight, I began to wonder if I were on the right street. The house, which I was ready to point out to the children hunched forward from their places in the back, was all white.

We were new in Los Angeles, and every day brought new and unusual experiences, but this seemed like the oddest happening to date. Driving home in disappointed silence, the truth suddenly dawned; it had been a movie set.

A month later it happened again.

This time, it was not a striped house, but a bustling Christmas-tree lot in mid-July. We didn't bother to spread the news in the neighborhood, and after dinner we played croquet in the front yard instead of revisiting the lot. We knew that by nightfall it would be bare.

In the city, a lot of things are backwards. Every place isn't Los Angeles, but every city has things that appear out of joint, cross-ways, full of paradox.

Man is crowded, but lonely.

He is rich, but poor.

He is busy, but bored.

He is surrounded by thirty-five institutions dedicated to his security—police, firemen, building inspectors, ambulances, help-line telephone numbers, public defenders, suicide-prevention bureaus—yet he is afraid, afraid even of the man across the street.

He has everything to do, yet nothing that really seems to matter in the long run.

He ignores religion, but is starved for God.

And don't tell him if he has any sense he'll blow the joint. He's not going to get out. He means to stay. But he needs someone to teach him how to live there, to coach him in the art of living and loving, to show him how to put his arms around the city where the significance of his being is evolving.

No one can predict the outcome of the American adventure,

29

but it will be settled in the city. That is where the people are now, and where they're going to be found in the future.

Rural America is becoming increasingly a fading memory. Most U.S. citizens are committed to urban life. They have values, priorities, loves, guilts, and desires for significance. They want their humanity to succeed. Meaningful religion seems to have gotten lost, or smashed, in the interplay of huge urban forces.

Lew and Carol Robinson were married eight years ago, a year before Lew finished law school in Columbus. Now his office is in the Tishman Building. Things are looking better all the time. His last new shirts cost fifteen dollars each. He works long hours, but that's okay because he never wanted to be anything except a lawyer. Working on cases where there's lots at stake—money, the firm's reputation, his own reputation—suits him perfectly. Carol runs the home. On days when she has help, she shops, plays par-three golf and does volunteer work. Joey is six. He is healthy and bright. He has learned to swim and idolizes Jerry West, star of the Lakers.

Carol was brought up in the Methodist Church and Lew has grown accustomed to writing "Episc." in the blank marked Religious Preference. At one time, he went to St. George's, or St. Gregory's or something like that. There's too much to do now to bother with church, except when Carol's parents are here from Ohio. What Lew likes, when he has time, is baroque music. He also thinks he'd like to join the Glider Club. He's a decent guy. He leaves the secretaries alone. Carol is still soft and interesting. I wouldn't have met the Robinsons if I hadn't stumbled onto Carol one afternoon in a hospital corridor. She was standing there with a doctor whom I know. She was crying when he beckoned to me. The first frightened words I heard her say were, "But he's only thirty-four!"

Ruby and Paul have no children. They live in the Valley and their icebox is always full of beer. Paul's a fisherman, and on weekends they take off for the San Bernardino Mountains. Paul works in an aircraft plant; Ruby works in a candy factory. Ruby used to attend Mass alone, but for the last two years, religion has not been mentioned between them. Sometimes she thinks about it after Paul has gone to sleep beside her, or when she notices a priest on the street. Neither cares much about expensive furniture, but boats are something else. Paul loves his boat, and Ruby loves Paul. Life is good, especially weekends! Paul has promised himself that one of these weekends he is going to get something off his mind, something that has been bothering him a long time. He's going to tell Ruby about his other family back in Davenport.

Sue is single. She's had one computer date which was surprisingly successful. She has a wonderful job and writes home to Duluth once a week. I met her in a neighborhood bookstore, when we found ourselves looking through the same poetry shelves.

"Do you like James Dickey's poems?" she asked pleasantly.

Five poets and twenty minutes later, I knew quite a lot about Sue, a girl with strong feelings about what matters in life and what doesn't.

When I asked about religion she said, "Religion is too busy looking at itself. It has forgotten the world."

These glimpses show us some of the people the city is filled with. They are people in pilgrimage, for the most part, who remain unaddressed, unhelped by Biblical faith. Bernard Via had a whole legion of them in mind when he wrote this.

> Dime-thin the walls
> Between the double-income couples
> That live eleven stories up
> Beside me.
>
> Dollar-thick the mood that
> Guarantees our privacy
> As undisturbed tenants
> Of an elevation
> That brings us no closer to God.

Some are trapped. In the fifties and sixties, cities were flooded by migration from Appalachia and the South. Once there, there was no other place to go except back. Return to small towns, though, with their post-office conversations and grocery-store charge accounts was about as thinkable as settling on the moon. Employment was a hundred times more plentiful in the city, and, for minorities, there was identity and commiseration. That was no small gain.

Most came to the city because that's where the action is. It's where the neon is, the noise, the experimentation, the stadiums, the museums, the airports, the paychecks, the night life, the industry, the votes, and the murders and the despair.

Does this mean that the future is to be molded and defined by people who, for the most part, believe that religious faith has little to contribute to what they're doing, feeling, and becoming, and by people who hold that a relationship with God is part of an abandoned small-town past with no bearing on the gut issues of urban society? Or does it mean that the church had better start digging the urban style?

Church membership is declining. Ninety-five percent of apartment dwellers never go near a church on Sunday or any other day. For most city dwellers, weekends are preempted as escape time—escape from the pressure of having to be at a certain place at a certain hour to do a certain thing. When death comes, many families now request, without embarrassment, "No funeral, thank you."

What's ahead? Is religion a defunct department of American life? Is the church capable of the renewal that will make its message congruent with a mobile, flexible man? Or is it urban man himself who has missed Dead Man's Curve and landed in a ditch of material confusion?

The city has indeed become the Secular City. That does not mean no-god. What it means is that there is a desperate need now to restate the relationship between God and man in co-creator terms. Urban man must be told that God is liberating Spirit, not confining obligation.

If city life seems turned around, upside down, full of contradictions, symbolized by striped houses and Christmas in July, think about the advent of the One whose life became the basis of a revolutionary hope. He was born in the simplest circumstances in a small Middle East country presided over by a puppet king. His human father was a carpenter. His birth went unnoticed and the first thirty years of His life were lived in a small town, in obscurity.

32

His career as a prophet was short-lived, and ended as the result of a conspiracy among certain urban leaders of religion who felt threatened by His teaching.

A Jew, He made it clear that His primary mission was to Jews, yet most of those who followed Him and attempted to implement His dream in the years following His death were not Jews.

He said the last will be first.

He said life begins in death.

He said enemies are to be loved.

He caused the lame to walk, the deaf to hear, the blind to see.

In His set-up, everything was backwards. In His world, every house was painted in stripes, and Christmas always came in summer.

That's what the city needs, someone who can reverse its priorities so men are more important than machines, commitment more important than comfort, and peace more important than profit.

War has been declared against urban poverty. It also must be declared against an urban life-style which lacks reference to God, and which underplays the urgency of a life purpose. If the man in Watts has a problem, so does the man in Trousdale Estates. His problem is the discovery of what lies beyond pleasure and safety. Once such needs are satisfied, there is an increasing amount of time left over for the question, "What's it all about, Alfie?"

When we are through claiming the world for ourselves, we begin a search for that which can claim us.

The church has been slow to grasp, understand, or to empathize with the urban style, with this new man in motion, caught up in the joy of experimentation and more concerned with the dilemmas of total society than the ethics of personal naughtiness—but dawn is coming.

The church has stopped being preoccupied with answering questions that no one is asking. It now recognizes what the city man wants to know is what to do with his creative instincts, how to organize his family life so that his home becomes more than a feeding station, how to conquer bigotry within himself and how to make the most of technological miracles without allowing them to robotize his feelings. The church knows he is more enraptured

by McLuhan than Malachi and more excited by an astronaut
dangling from a golden tether in space than by a story about
a golden calf.

Man also is called to re-examine the Christian faith in its contemporary expressions. If he will include, among his top priorities,
the grace of listening, the church can help him come to know
who he is. It can help equip him to cope with a world engulfed in radical change. It can help him achieve a perspective that keeps the visible and invisible worlds in balance. It can
furnish him a basis for hope, even in the face of massive cruelties
and frustrations. It can help turn him from part of the problem
into part of the answer.

4

"There's a Lion Loose in My Airplane!"

Two Flying Tiger pilots narrowly escaped injury yesterday
when a lion escaped from its cage during a cargo flight. The
tower had difficulty believing the nature of the distress signal
when it was reported, but instructed emergency procedures
when the radio picked up the snarls of the wild animal. The
plane landed safely at Lowry Field, Denver.

Los Angeles Times

AMERICA, in the latter half of what were to have been the soaring
sixties, became a society of snarls. At times, the snarling and
spitting could be more accurately called blood-chilling roars. As
the seventies open, the byword is *polarization* as generations,
races, protesters, and haves-versus-have-nots square off against
one another and paw the dirt.

Violent solutions to human problems have produced a cacophony
of discord which makes the "Star Spangled Banner" sound as if

it were being listened to against the background of a tree-snapping hurricane. It has become a time of anger, anarchy and challenge to every virtue upon which America's self-understanding is believed to rest. In the words of Jeremiah, the soaring sixties became, near their close, "a time to destroy."

At first, the American church seemed to be identified more closely with the problem than the answer, with traditional speaking rather than sensitive listening. Early in the decade the church tended to discount reports of loose lions, and argued instead for routine flight patterns, patience, reasonableness; then it began to listen to what a society in labor was saying.

Organized Christianity now has been fully penetrated by the noises of social, technological, moral and intellectual revolution. Many church members have been frightened by this dive into a sea of controversy, and have called for a retrenchment from programs that have church buildings resounding with the noise of Black-Manifesto debates, Head Start classes, literacy instruction, housing seminars, and hostel-type accommodations for people en-route to a Washington march. There appears to be no turning back. Made leaner by diminished rolls, the church is, nevertheless, increasingly more toughly disciplined, committed, and influential in the shaping of destiny.

It is hard to get the volume of conscience turned up high enough to pick up the messages through the heavy layers of insulation and isolation which have shielded the church from the world for so long. How can it have empathy, or insight into the feelings of families who live in houses they share with rats? How can it know the pain of the city from the vantage of the vaulted freeway? How does one register, on the sensors of his spirit, the hopelessness of slum life, if he never enters the slums? How can a citizen with three automobiles, who pays more per month in income taxes than his own father ever made in salary, enter the grief of the uneducated and the unemployed—whose main interest is not advancement but survival?

Are not large sectors of urban America crying out in one way or another for rescue, for deliverance, for some kind of faith to live by? Are men shouting, "Mayday! Mayday! There's a lion loose in my airplane"?

35

One of the things urban men are saying (whether for good or for evil), is that they prefer to live together in great metropolitan centers rather than in small towns. They are saying also that living in the city is costly. It costs men the healing associations of trees and sky, streams and distances. It costs them their identity as persons. Sometimes, it costs in the feeling of being needed and of being closely bound up with, and into, the larger family of Man.

Most of us like the city. We like its motion and power, its hum and action, its universities, lights, and luxuries. If the city extracts its price in terms of frustration, impersonality, crime, fear of one another, and the high cost of getting the plumbing fixed, it also gives generously of itself in the form of a wider dimension of existence through a greater sweep across the scenery of life and opportunity, and a chance to explore and exploit life to the full. I hear voices saying that most of us love the city and intend to stay here, but help us. Help us not to be destroyed by its roar, its cleavages, its ruthlessness, its capacity for ugliness and killing, its suffocations and its potential for crushing that within us which is meant to be gentle and good.

A funeral service was held for a young soldier who came home from military service depressed and confused. After several months of trying to get himself emotionally righted, he took his own life. The memorial was attended by a large crowd and was held in a stuffy, small urban chapel on a warm September afternoon. Afterwards, the cortege made a twenty-mile drive to a national cemetery and, to avoid the busier roads, was routed through a rural countryside. The azure sky and the soft, late-summer air was silky upon our faces. The rough rock-exposed hillsides were dotted with motionless sheep. Each mile, that day, brought an added increment of comfort. Earth alone had achieved what words had been unable to do.

People who live in Southern California are able to enjoy a whole panorama of benedictions—groves, gardens, a valentine border of mountains, sea, sand, oleander and tropical starlight. Still, for many, life in the city is unrelieved gimcrack—selling-out signs, trash-strewn vacant lots, and junkie jungles. There is the cry— Help us live in the city! Help us live here in decency, in the security of family love, in self-respect and mutual responsibility. Help us to make and to use the city as fulfillment, rather than as a concrete anvil upon which our spirits are bludgeoned to death.

Urban man is also saying something like this, "I rejoice in the miracles of science, but science is not my saviour."

Science does not pretend to be a saviour. No real scientist ever pretended that science is a substitute for love, another name for God, or a basis for forgiveness. As we are determined to live in the city, so are we determined to milk technology for all it is worth. We see no reason to be ashamed of that. Rather than being ashamed, we are grateful the mind of man is so versatile that the prospect of a healthier, more significant life together is increased by each discovery. Urban man is not choosing science over faith, but is saying to most institutional religion, "Come, join the present age. Speak to us in a language we understand. Do not stand in the middle of the road blocking traffic—defensive, parochial, dogmatic, petty and ignorant of the dynamisms that have made today one of the most exciting periods in which men have lived. Get with it!" To the church the world is saying, "Examine your hymns, your aims, your spirit, your claims, your names, your unity, your demands of those who identify themselves with you and what you give. The church, if it is to be in dialogue with a world (which at times resembles a zoo just being organized), if it is to contribute to the redemption of the world's life and protect the humanity of man, must exhibit new relevance, consistency, vocabulary, and imagination. It must lead if it wants men to follow. If it will not lead, others will. Having listened, the church may qualify itself to speak.

Churches, from Philadelphia to Salt Lake City, are stumbling about trying to reach outside of stained glass enclaves. Where the desire is real, the way opens easily into the social wounds of the city. The recipe is fantastically simple—act upon your faith, do something that's needed. Examine the part of the world you know best—the place where God has put you, the people, the problems, the smells, the hungers, the puzzles, the blemishes and the burdens, the anxieties and the pent-up anger you already look at every day, but maybe do not see. Study that world; brood over its brokenness and distortion and you'll hear a lion roaring.

Proverbs 26:13 has a line which served as the title of a novel, *There's a Lion in the Streets*. It refers to a man who, afraid to cope with the tough demands of life, came back with a scarey tall-tale excuse for inaction, saying it wasn't safe to go out there. Perhaps it isn't safe, but the pilot wasn't lying when he called the Tower, and the world isn't either.

5

Two People Met at the Water Cooler

Two women met by a well,
And laid their pitchers on the edge.
Each one's face was stained with tears,
And one looked to the other and said,
"They executed my son today.
They nailed him to a cross on Calvary.
He died a common criminal's death,
While they let a murderer go free."
And then she looked up and said,
"My son's name was Jesus."
The other woman then replied,
As the words broke through her strife,
"My son died this morning also,
But with a rope he took his life."
And then she faced the woman
Whose feeling was the same.
"My son died this morning also.
Judas was his name."

JOHN ABBOTT

IN THE MIDDLE of the day, a woman came to draw water from Jacob's well. There she met Jesus who had stopped to rest in the middle of a journey of his own. Jesus, coming up from the south, was headed for Galilee, the northern province of Palestine. The most direct route led through the middle political state known as Samaria.

He knew he was passing through unfriendly territory. He knew, when he asked the Samaritan woman for a drink of water, it was a violation of custom, but He is not remembered for His timidity. It was the woman more than the water that interested Him.

John never merely tells a story. He tells it as an excuse to teach. If he writes concerning the multiplication of loaves and fishes, it is in order to explain Jesus as the Bread of Life. If he describes the healing of a blind man, it is an excuse to discuss him as the Light of the World. If he tells of the raising of Lazarus, it is as prologue to a discussion of Jesus as the Resurrection Hope.

The story, retold in modern dress, might begin like this. Two people met one day in front of the water-cooler on the ninth floor of the Union Oil Building. . . .

Here is a pattern, a pattern of communication which helps us understand and enlarge upon the man-God relation.

First, there is opening. "Please, may I have a drink of water?"

This is the testing for response. The Samaritan woman is surprised, relieved. The look on the Asker's face assures her there is welcome in His heart as well as His words. It's still nothing more than "Hello," or "It's a lovely day," or "Gee, it's hot."

The next movement is the encounter. "Bring your husband, I would like to meet him."

"I'm sorry, I have no husband."

"That's right," says the Traveler with both humor and sympathy in His voice. "You've lived with five men, now you are living with a sixth, but even he's not your husband because you are not married to him. That's a true statement—'I have no husband.' "

There must have been embarrassing silence after this remark. It included the pain which often accompanies honesty, but there was more than honesty. There was caring, too, and a readiness to understand, to go forward from this point to something more. Often we find ourselves unable to cross such a boundary into another self. We are afraid. We remain lonely and outside.

But He entered. He crossed over, and the woman's reaction

39

was the familiar one—evasion. She ignored His probe and sought to engage this Stranger in a discussion of how Jews and Samaritans differ in their habits of worship. Was one mountain more sacred than another? How did He, a Jew, feel about that often discussed point?

Jesus' reply that God is Spirit, and that those who worship Him must worship Him in spirit and in truth, rather than from habit or at any divinely-commanded spot, left her speechless.

At this point, the disciples suddenly return, having come back from Sychar where they had gone to buy supplies. The interruption causes the woman to flee in such excitement that she leaves her water jar. Back to her village she hurries, saying with excitement, "Come, see a man who told me all I ever did!"

Assign your own title to step four. Call it self-discovery, faith, renewal. Whatever name you choose, it means triumph through the recovery of a sense of personal worth—something to be talked about, sung about, remembered, lived.

The steps include movement, opening to encounter, encounter to evasion and evasion to self-acceptance.

Human understanding begins this way. A boy helps a girl with her coat and a circuit closes. We hold out our hands to someone by a smile, or a remark about having seen snowcapped Baldy on a day of distances. We keep ourselves protected and defended, but fling out little straws upon the wind.

"Please, a drink of water . . .," we say several times daily.

Fred Buechner imagines a deserted railroad station.

Let us say that one of the people is you, and the other is a stranger. The silence between you is very deep, so deep that you can almost hear it, but there is no convention that says you must speak to a stranger in a public place, so it is not an embarrassing silence like the silence on occasions where human beings are expected to speak. In fact the truth of it is that for you the stranger is hardly a human being; he is a face dimly seen, a dark shape sitting on a bench or leaning against the wall. The silence, the emptiness, the preoccupation with your own thoughts and your own waiting, separate you from him as fully as light-years of space separate stars. The mystery of who you are—your loves and fears and dreams—are hidden from him as the mystery of who he is, is hidden from you; and if somebody asked you later if there was anyone else there with you you might say, "No. At least I don't think so. I'm not sure."

Then maybe . . . on impulse, you speak—"Hi . . . It's a long wait."

It's where love begins, but if it is to become love, it must travel from, "Hi," to deep encounter. Must it also cross lands of evasion? Probably, since it is easy for us to dodge, shift, hide. Try to talk about something else. Psychiatrists say difficulties involving sexual compatibility, ninety-five times out of a hundred, are a facade for anxieties about self-worth and dreams, for wanting to be understood in non-mechanical terms. All men are experts in evasion because the alternative is pain and risk. We are afraid to allow strangers in for a look around, but, when we do, a band begins to play and new freedoms are born.

The opening can be all sorts of things—a walk along a beach, a verse from the Bible, a moment of quiet, another human being in whose face we see the sadness of God, or talking with a child about death. The city, with all its urban wounds, is filled with openings. We're apt to bump into God on almost any street corner and hear Him say, "Please, a drink of water."

Much of the church's fumbling, as we have just seen, is the result of too much talking and too little listening—too much monologue, too little dialogue.

Listening and love are closely-related enterprises. Love involves living outside ourselves, projecting ourselves into the needs and dreams of those around us, but it won't happen unless we listen.

Consider this letter.

Dear Folks,
Thank you for everything, but I am going to Chicago and try and start some kind of a new life.
You asked me why I did those things and why I gave you so

41

much trouble, and the answer is easy for me to give you, but I am wondering if you will understand.

Remember when I was about six or seven and I used to want you to just listen to me? I remember all the nice things you gave me for Christmas and my birthday and I was really happy with the things—about a week—at the time I got the things, but the rest of the time during the year I really didn't want presents. I just wanted all the time for you to listen to me like I was somebody who felt things, too, because I remember even when I was young I felt things. But you said you were busy.

Mom, you are a wonderful cook, and you had everything so clean and you were tired so much from doing all those things that made you busy; but you know something, Mom? I would have liked crackers and peanut butter just as well if you had only sat down with me a while during the day and said to me, "Tell me all about it so I can maybe help you understand!"

And when Donna came I couldn't understand why everyone made so much fuss because I didn't think it was my fault that her hair is curly and her skin so white, and she doesn't have to wear glasses with such thick lenses. Her grades were better, too, weren't they?

If Donna ever has children, I hope you will tell her to just pay some attention to the one who doesn't smile very much because that one will really be crying inside. And when she's about to bake six dozen cookies, to make sure first, that the kids don't want to tell her about a dream or a hope or something, because thoughts are important too, to small kids even though they don't have so many words to use when they tell about what they have inside them.

I think that all the kids who are doing so many things that grownups are tearing out their hair worrying about are really looking for somebody who will have time to listen a few minutes and who really and truly will treat them as they would a grownup who might be useful to them, you know—polite to them. If you folks had ever said to me: "Pardon me" when you interrupted me, I'd have dropped dead!

42

If anybody asks you where I am, tell them I've gone looking for somebody with time because I've got a lot of things I want to talk about.

Love to all,
YOUR SON

Here's a prayer.

> Lord, forgive me!
> Forgive me for being too busy
>   to realize that my wife has feelings, too;
>   too busy
> to let my child interrupt me while I read
>   the paper or watch TV—
>   too busy
> to try to understand the complaints of my
>   associates at work.
> Help me today, while there is still time,
>   to listen.

If the gospel is to take hold, to reach behind men's masks and to begin to refresh the lives of intimacy-starved and faith-hungry people, then the church must match its preaching and affirmation with the kind of active, non-judgmental listening without which understanding is impossible.

Faith is meeting. It is God and man crossing the threshold of each other, passing from politeness to embrace. To encounter another person is to be changed by that person. To meet God is to be changed by Him.

The church needs an experience of the message powerful enough to make her forget her jars. If living faith sweeps in to animate her aspirations and move her to action, there will be many in search of direction who will do exactly that. Come and see!

6

Love Is Communication: Communication Is Love

A new communications satellite has been proposed to the COMSAT Corporation. It would have communications capacity 25 times that of Early Bird. One of the satellites could relay 6,000 two-way telephone calls, or 12 color television programs, or any combinations of communications transmissions. The power of the satellite will be so great that commercial quality reception can be obtained with inexpensive ground antennas as small as 30 feet. This will enable small, emerging nations to join the network more quickly and at far less expense.

Monday Morning

A TELEVISION commercial pictures two large pieces of wood being glued together. The glue is so strong the pieces of wood, when suspended between two sawhorses, are able to support even the weight of a large piano. Today, we are looking for glue that will hold the world together. We can step that need down a bit and say, before we get to that problem, we seek something to hold the nation together. Step it down once more, and let's admit we are looking for some principle or energy that can enable us simply to hold ourselves together.

In Colossians, Paul, after speaking of Jesus as "the image of the invisible God," says of Him, "He is before all things, and in him all things hold together" (1:17 RSV). This chapter asks why that is so, and how it is so.

Jesus once asked a sick man, "Do you want to be made whole?" That is still the king of questions—wholeness, integrity, a life of peace rather than of pieces. A wheel, which turns at high speed, must be balanced or it will shudder and fight with

44

itself and fly apart. A nation, too, must hold certain values in common, or it cannot remain a nation. The earth has its sun, the body its brain. Man, as spirit, needs a Christ, and man as a social animal, who must live with other men, and by them discover himself, must also find a unifying principle for his life with others.

Love is that principle. Love is the heart of communication, and communication is the heart of community. If we can love, we can communicate, and if we can communicate, we can love. If we can *both* love and communicate, we can live. Learned communication with God will enable us to do a better job of communicating with each other, because in God's presence our disguises and defenses have to be abandoned. Liberated from lies and illusions about ourselves, we become both more accessible and more ready to reach out.

Communication would seem to be easier than ever in this age of technological wonders. The report from COMSAT, reproduced in the headnote is good news internationally, but it doesn't help a family that cannot talk together, even though it lives under the same roof. Nor is it enough to heal a city or nation struggling with alienation between old and young, black and white, city and suburb, though television has greatly helped to make us more aware of each other as persons.

The difficulty we are in is not hard to understand. We are now a pluralistic people, and there is no longer a common body of knowledge. Early in our career as a society, the Bible was a universal literature. If everyone did not know its contents, at least everyone was expected to have general familiarity with it. There were the classics, *Aesop's Fables, Good Housekeeping* magazine and a limited set of scientific ideas. There was the flag, Thanksgiving Day and the Twentieth Century Limited that would take you at blazing speed from Chicago to New York between sunset and sunrise. Increasingly, though, we have less common information with which to identify. We have become two hundred million people, more secular, more diverse and crowded into cities; but often with little to say to one another. Belief in God, regardless of what the polls say, is up for grabs. I would hesitate to call belief in God any real adhesive with

power to hold our present society together. With the urbaniza-
tion of life, we also observe a vacuum developing between
political decisions and the people. Frequently people withdraw,
or do not take part beyond the casting of their annual ballot,
because going to a meeting at which some important matter is
being considered is so hard—finding the right street, finding a
place to park, thinking it isn't safe to venture out.

We hear much use of *consensus,* but there is not much consensus today about life, morality, or anything, and that crisis of
meaning has produced a crisis of communication. People have more
money, but less joy in common, and less feeling of need for one
another. Even within universities, there is often difficulty in
talking to each other because knowledge is highly specialized.
Each discipline has its own language. Each wants to find out
where it fits in cracking the code of a truly human humanity.

We hear much about the servant role of the church. This is
right for Jesus regularly referred to Himself as a servant. The
church is in the world in His stead. If the church really is the
servant of men, it must do something to improve and to enlarge
communication between people and between structures. It would
be difficult to exaggerate the importance of such a ministry,
if our formula is true, that communication, when it is real,
produces love, and that love produces community and peace.

One problem is that we are forced to rely too much on the
power of words, both written and spoken, to convey meaning and
carry the burden of understanding. Words are often poor vehicles.
They are clumsy, frequently misinterpreted, and often do more
harm than good.

Will Rogers said, "I never met a man I didn't like." He meant
that given the chance really to experience another person—any
person—it is relatively easy to learn to love him within a short
time. It takes getting behind mere word sounds and behind
masks we wouldn't dare leave the house without. It requires ex-
posing the deeper person. This often doesn't happen between
people. The hidden person never gets revealed. The words fly
back and forth but they never cross.

My father-in-law, before his retirement, was an engineer who
supervised the installation of mechanical equipment in large dairy

farms in the Middle West. One day, he was sent to consult with the managers of a large farm operated by Trappist monks near Dubuque, Iowa. The brothers lived under vows of silence and were allowed to speak to each other, or to outsiders, only at certain times or under special circumstances. Those discussing the problems of the farm with the consultants, which included my father-in-law, were, of course, freed from such restraints, at least for the duration of the consultation. There would be little chance of accomplishing the improvement program if they weren't. The visiting engineers were told, as they toured the farm, that they were not to speak to the others who would be working quietly at their chores. This went as planned, until the group unexpectedly popped around the corner of a barn, to find two surprised brothers, each holding the end of a hose, engaged in a vigorous water fight while still holding to the vow to remain silent.

A housewife is in the kitchen in lowering darkness. It has been a tiring, frustrating day. Her numerous chores and active children have sapped her strength and patience. Now the final meal is over, and she is stuck with the job of cleaning up the kitchen. Her husband, who has been at his air-conditioned office through the day doing interesting things—having lunch at the Corkscrew, and dealing with adults rather than kids—is sitting off in the living room, smoking his pipe and reading the evening paper. The wife feels put upon, even abused, as she ends her day in the scullery. To register her frustration, she bangs the pots and pans in such a way as to send a message into the living room, where her mate is puffing on his pipe and reading about what happened to his team. He hears her message and translates it correctly. He resents it because he's been out battling the world, too. Now he feels he is entitled to some moments of rest. He responds to the pan-banging with an angry rustling of the paper.

Thus do we signal each other. We signal by smiles, by the inflections of our voices, by the tautness of our face muscles. We signal by heavy, resentment-filled silence. We speak by hand-shakes, kisses, and hugs. An article about the Kennedys says they have always been a great family to touch each other, and that in sorrow they helped to make each other brave by touching. We communicate by our dress, the way we walk, the way we

47

laugh, the way we shut the door. We communicate with our eyes, with our hands, our chins.

Sometimes, we want to communicate and can't. We want to be known and to be understood, but our feelings are too elusive, unclear or protected. We are afraid of being laughed at or criticized, so we stay concealed.

Youth now is communicating to older persons in all kinds of ways. The most eloquent medium is music. How often they confess, "I can't talk to my parents; I can't reach them. They don't try to understand. They don't want to understand. It's hopeless. They're afraid of the drug thing, or somebody getting pregnant outside of marriage, or my hair, or my skirt length, but they don't know the real me—they don't know the real me at all!"

The civil rights movement broke apart on the same rocks. The laws went on the books, traditional discriminations were abandoned, but ships were passing in the night, and there was little communication on the level where it mattered most. It was arms-length ethics. Because communication on this level failed, black people turned to each other and decided that there was only one choice left—separateness; and how can one make the most of separateness without staying at the bottom of the pile?

Does the church have a ministry of communication? It is her greatest ministry, her most helpful service toward the lifting of society from the ditch, binding up the wounds, and enabling the journey to go on.

The church does this by helping people to understand that persons and personal relationships are the most important things on earth, even more important than good health. When Paul said that love is the greatest of all virtues, he hit the middle of the target. People cannot love unless they can communicate. If they do not honestly communicate, their love turns out to be forty-nine-cent jewelry.

In Jesus all things hold together, because in Him we find the courage to reach out to touch, to love without fear. Loving, we become whole.

The church fosters communication when it links people together in commitment, seals them together through agony and joy, good times and bad. The church ministers to men's need to communicate when it keeps saying to them that they are the children of God created for fellowship with Him—not for lonely existence on a derelict star.

The church also helps to create men of sensitive imagination and service by holding up the life, death, and Resurrection of Jesus. This enables persons to make contact, for here each recognizes something of himself.

Love is communication. Communication is love. Both statements are true. Both appropriate the power of faith—both affirm a confidence that when men open themseives up to God and desire to relate to Him and to His purposes, they have a basis for understanding each other that will not let them down, and which, in the fullness of history, will make them one.

A man returned for a reunion of college friends. Apart for thirty years, several did not know who he was as he walked into the room. Instead of disclosing his identity, he went out to the car and brought in his son, now about the age he had been when they had known him. Recognition was instant.

In Jesus, we recognize the Father. This is the first step toward freedom—the freedom to know, to forgive, and to love both ourselves and those of whom we can say, because of Him, we are strangers no more.

II
FREEWAYS ARE GREAT IF YOU KNOW WHERE YOU'RE GOING

7

Don't Leave Town on Friday Afternoon

We are the ones who have torn ourselves away from our
Creator and have taken flight. We are the ones who, like
sheep, have gone astray, turning each one to his own way.
We are the ones who have not tolerated God's Lordship and
are now in varying stages of escape. We are the fugitives!
We are the vagabonds! We are the Gingerbread People!

JAMES PECK

FRIDAY AFTERNOON, the freeways become impossible. Everybody
and his brother is on the road, headed for the open country
and the feel of tree bark, the sound of splashing water and out-
board motors, the delight of dirt paths without stoplights. Weekends are for washing the city out of the system. Five days are
enough; then, it's time to get away, if you can, out where the
sky turns inky black at night, and you fall asleep to the music
of the wind.

Is that the whole truth about our weekly exodus from the city,
or is urban man's flight from the city symptomatic of his hunger
to escape?

Running never has been much of an answer, but it always
has been a temptation with flaming red hair. Whether we are
homesick GIs, businessmen staring into hard decisions, or part-
ners in marriage, there is always a temptation to run, to slam
the door, to crawl into a bottle, to seek refuge in a world of
illusion, to trade responsibility for release, and to imagine "how
happy we would be if we all lived in a yellow submarine."
Mescaline, eroticism and TV's dramas of distraction are all part of
an effort to find a substitute universe. It's a fake. Happiness by

53

consumption has its inevitable disillusionments. Over the years the wonder just seems to go out of Wonder Bread, and Marlboro country turns out to be just another prairie without indoor plumbing.

Running from sorrow, the pretending that avoids the work of grief (which, if we will endure it, will heal us), is another detour.

We flee smaller problems. A minister dreams of another church where people aren't so difficult. Half his heart says, "Leave!" The other half says, "Stay!" We do wrong. We blunder, sin, hunt for avenues of escape. We can't understand ourselves. We want to get away from ourselves. Run! But where? The son of a hard-driving physician was critically hurt in a sports car accident. In the hospital dining room—in a building where he was used to spending long days, and nights as well—the doctor meditated upon his profession and upon the life of his son.

"I'm sure I go at it so hard because then I don't have time left over to think about what it all means," he said.

Run! Don't stop—that could be fatal.

With national questions, too, we are tempted to take a trip instead of facing our troubles and demanding in God's name that they surrender to our resolve to overcome them. History, like our own lives, has a way of racking along for what seems like an interminable time. Nothing varies very much. There are no cruel defeats, no smashing victories, just morning, noon, night and morning again. Then there come from out of silence, a few brief, powerful moments producing an assassination and all of a sudden life is changed.

In the United States, we have come to the point where two kinds of running have discredited themselves. One running is represented by riot—a blind, uncaring disregard for everything except our own bitterness and hostility. Protest is a proud part of our history. "Taxation without representation is tyranny!" was a fine shout. "We shall overcome!" is another. The upheaval over race had to be. Health was impossible without the death of an old half-corrupt order. It is to our national credit that we openly chose to suffer our way through transition instead of pulling the covers over our heads, waiting for problems to disappear.

54

It is impossible to argue or to reason with a rioter. At some point, protest may stop serving as the effective use of power and become mindless retreat, become the "sleep of reason."

Another kind of running is the politics of repression—the idea that if the strong get tough enough with the weak and use enough force, threat and punishment, we will be able to look out and see doves of peace alighting upon our red, white and blue rooftops. This may not be running, but it is hiding, even so. We cannot pile on more and more bandages to heal infection. Something powerful must be injected into the public bloodstream and allowed to go to work. If we are to save America from apartheid, we must save our cities from decay, from assuming the shape of black hate-centers surrounded by white borders.

At last we are awake—trembling, but awake. In a sense we have been running from the crisis, but the crossroads have been reached; and we seek grace, now, that we may not flee the thunder and lightning but fly bravely through it toward a new unity and fresh destiny.

There is still another running—the running the shepherds did that first Christmas night when they went with haste to where Jesus lay sleeping. It is running forward, not backward. It is a running that means glad excitement, help on the way, eagerness, ministry. It is the double-quick pace of the Christian in a troubled time. It is running which means that we affirm our existence, celebrate it and welcome the future. In the story of the Prodigal Son, it is the father who runs. (God running—think of that!) He fell on the boy's neck and kissed him, saying, "I'm glad you came back!" At first freedom had meant for him nothing more than freedom from his father's house—freedom to do as he pleased, to be out from under it all. This was freedom misunderstood. The man who cannot attain freedom in the circumstances in which he finds himself cannot hope to attain it simply by changing places.

During my boyhood, I had many jobs—cleaning a barbershop before school, carrying the *Des Moines Register,* working at a fruit and vegetable counter, serving as flunky at a bottling plant. I'll never forget my first day there. Steam was used for cleaning and sterilizing the bottles for Coca-Cola as they rattled along on tiny conveyor tracks prior to reaching the filling machine. It was contained in large tanks. When the pressure became too high, a release valve was set to open and exhaust enough steam to drop the pressure to within safe limits. Whenever that happened, the valve made a loud, hissing noise. When it occurred that first Monday morning, an older employee yelled, "Run! She's going to blow up!" It was enough warning for me. I left my place with the speed of a missile and didn't turn around until I was a block away. There I waited for the plant to go flying into the air. Five minutes later, I walked sheepishly back to my place.

Today, we have a choice. We can run like deer—afraid of changes we do not understand, afraid of death, afraid of people not like ourselves, afraid of the world—or run, shepherd-style toward them, toward tomorrow, and toward that better day, we call the Kingdom of God. One will make us a truant; the other a pioneer.

8

Roses Still Are Delivered to Marilyn Monroe

... Our little lives, our big problems—these we place
  upon Thy altar!
Brood over our spirits, Our Father,
Blow upon whatever dream Thou hast for us
That there may glow once again upon our hearths
The light from Thy altar.
Pour out upon us whatever our spirits need of
  shock, of lift, of release,
That we might find strength for these days—
Courage and hope for tomorrow. ...

HOWARD THURMAN

MARILYN MONROE is buried next door to our church in West-wood. Roses are still delivered three times a week. Tourists are often seen strolling in the small graveyard, pausing to take pictures of a small bronze plaque which reads MARILYN MONROE 1926-1962.

In the fifties, her name was as well known as that of the president of the United States. Her death, from an overdose of sleeping tablets, shocked a pizzazz-minded world which decided anyone with as much pizzazz as hers had to be public property. In her life, the sensuous side of our culture and the deep hunger of a human being for identity and happiness met head on. Culture won.

Marilyn's spirit broods over the neighborhood—the spirit of a stunning girl who wrote in a notebook, while shooting *Let's Make Love,* "What am I afraid of? Do I think I can't act? I know I can act but I am afraid. I am afraid and I should not be and I must not be." It is the spirit of a woman who, in spite of beauty, brains, fame and fortune, died a lonely death on a battle-field of silk sheets.

Whether or not her death was the result of suicide is disputed. *Accident* sounds better and makes all our tragedies slightly more bearable. *Suicide* is a raw word out of the Northwest, making ice out of our tears and turning our hearts abjectly dumb.

Still most of us, at some time, toy with the idea of suicide. We wonder if we would be capable of either the courage or the desperation or a combination of the two. Would it wind up pushing us over the cliff into a delicious oblivion? Each year, hundreds, many of them youths in their teens, have faced this possibility and decided on death.

In one way, Marilyn's decision is none of our business. The question she struggled with on that harsh, unforgettable August night was, "Why go on?" Why dream and try in such an ambiguous universe? Why go on masquerading, pretending there is a reference, a larger significance, if the whole thing is celluloid?

Albert Camus, a Monroe contemporary, debated the question and decided the only justification he could find was the personal dignity involved in the fight itself. The audience he commanded,

57

over his own brief span, is evidence that many agreed with the idea that suicide is a fairly decent solution to the riddle of existence, unless one is able to identify with some believable purpose.

Like a good woman, a good reason to live may be hard to find. "Why go on?" might be called the adult version of the *why* with which many childhood sentences begin. Suicide may not be the result of forty-two pills. You can be dead just walking around.

On Easter, this *why* dresses up and goes to church. It sits politely, waiting to be answered, yet knows its question will remain untouched. Other days, it takes the form of vocational boredom, walks with hopeless eyes along broken sidewalks of the black community, or hangs darkly in the air of the home for the retired. Another version of it, Roy Fairchild has dubbed the "suburban sadness."

> The despair may be less transparent but is more profound in Transurbia because American mythology has contended that here, once you arrive, you would find a constant level of happiness. Yet one finds in the suburb a pervasive sense of "stuckness"—stuckness with one's job, one's spouse, one's community round. We see a low-keyed monotony which pervades gardening, weekending, and community participation. These activities soon become a matter of duty rather than joy. Increasing numbers of men and women are creating emergencies and artificial spurs in their lives, many through sex, to manufacture a sense of drama and bite. This is not the occasional wildness which all human beings crave but an obsessive form of risk-taking and distraction.

Why? Beyond the idealism of early life, what's the rationale for a life that hungers to be prolonged?

Christianity has something important to say about this search. It is an alternative to suicide, a rationale for being, though at times the trail seems to fade off into the weeds. It does not help to say that the Christian faith is the answer, or that a person must be stupid or stubborn if he does not recognize it or subscribe to it. James Pike was correct when he said the age cries out for fewer beliefs but more belief. It does help, though, to recognize that Jesus is primarily the clue, the clue that enables many persons, day after day, to face life with courage and expectation. In the darkness, a small piece of light shines.

The gospel affirms two things. First, it says life can be meaningful enough to make us want it to continue. Second, it promises us that it will. Death is not the final sentence in the book.

Despite the difficulties involved in such faith, it is more than wishful thinking. It is a voice shouting yes! Still, it cannot be proved, either what the Voice says, or even if there is a Voice at all.

Faith is a gamble. Life, says its Author, is neither patently ridiculous, nor obviously fair. Rain falls on the just and the unjust. The kingdom does not come through observation. Confronted by a scorecard of evil, Jesus simply responded, "Now I'll ask *you* one." Life becomes significant only as we abandon ourselves to the possibility that it is. Only by faith can a man say, with Studdert-Kennedy, "These clouds are lies. . . . The blue sky is the Truth." Who will climb a mountain on a thread, knowing that, included in such risk, is the chance of winding up looking a fool?

Cynicism is sin, but we are apt to equate it naively with just the good old tough facts. A police officer found a man ready to leap from the San Francisco Bay Bridge.

"Stop!" he called to the man who stood there just inches from death. "You've got a lot to live for!"

A bargain was struck. Each would take five minutes to state a case for the worthwhileness or futility of life. According to the story, following the exchange of arguments, they locked arms and jumped together.

Despair has its opposition, too. In Edwin O'Connor's story about a dying priest, the narrator says, "[He] surprised me by telling me, with a little smile, that now that he was going, he wanted desperately to stay.

" 'A single memory can do it', he said.

"And I suppose he was right. The memory of an instant—of a smile, of leaf-smoke on a sharp fall day, of a golden streak across a rain-washed morning, of a small boy seated alone on the sea-

59

shore, solemnly building his medieval moated castles—just this one, single, final flash of memory can be enough to make us want to stay forever. . . ."

Who does not envy the lock on meaning of the astronaut who said, after a pioneer space flight, "This is something I would gladly give my life for"?

Joshua was so busy fighting for God he asked the sun not to go down until his mission had been accomplished. People in love are so consumed with one another, they ask the sun not to come up. Will Durant confessed to me, during my college days, "I would gladly give up everything I own in exchange for ten more years of life to go on with my work." He got those years and his completed history of civilization, a masterful achievement. Of eighty-six-year-old Frank Laubach, developer of the most successful literacy movement in history, an acquaintance said, "He is always deep in the present."

There is a difference between this kind of intensity and the success Marilyn Monroe came, for good reason, to despise. "Fame," she said, in an interview with a reporter from *Life*, "warms you a bit, but the warming is temporary. Fame will go by, and so long, I've had you, fame. If it goes by, I've always known it was fickle. So, at least it's something I experienced, but that's not where I live."

The love of even one other person is sufficient to turn fifteen minutes into a roaring miracle. A man was trying to comfort his friend whose engagement to a girl had just ended. "Women are like streetcars," he said, "There'll always be another one along in a few minutes." Anyone who has been really in love knows that that is a lie. It is failure to understand the extent with which one human being can represent the totality of joy to another. Still, no one can reach this conclusion, or implant this desire. The will to survive may be basic instinct, but the judgment that life is wonderful is something we opt for along the highway of freedom, and Christians are called to help the world choose. Unless there is this kind of appetite or feeling of realization, discussion about life's continuation is of no consequence.

A cartoon shows a man and a boy standing outside a sagging ghetto dwelling. Says the father, his arms about the boy's shoulders,

"Son, someday this will all be yours." If eternal life is a message about duration only, it could become a communiqué from hell. If, on the other hand, we are able by the grace of God to affirm enduring beauty and value in the absence of supporting evidence, even against contradictory evidence, we leap not to death but to life.

Once such a love affair with life is under way, the idea of Resurrection becomes a matter of genuine desire. Resurrection involves an even more outlandish risk. Who can believe it and on what grounds? The Carpenter's words and the empty tomb are convincing to only a few. More see life as a game of poker with a few large winnings early in the evening, but a midnight exit for all in boxes instead of barrels.

Faith argues that life survives because God survives. God transcends the boundaries of the situation, as does His love. The Christian, knowing this, raises his hand as if he's heard enough. "Stop the world," he says, "I want to get on!"

The really persuasive evidence of life beyond death is neither buttercups in the spring, nor the historical data of a museum, nor sentences in a book. It is rather a resurrection quality in people whose names we know and into whose faces we can look.

The message of the New Testament is that eternal life is available to men, and that the source of its breadth and strength is the God of life, to whom the Christ-event points. It says we can't appreciate the options apart from Him. The gospel tells us to fall in love, be prepared to be swept off our feet by the wonder and the danger of life. Have eyes for its motion, ears for its music, taste for its richness and desperate pleas for help. Don't ask or expect to have all its secrets divulged. Risk ourselves to the unknown. Be fascinated by the thought that we can become exhibits of renaissance ourselves!

The light of Marilyn's life flickered and failed at the point of the second *why,* and we struggle with our *why's,* too. Why give life our vote? Why be optimistic about tomorrow? On what basis do we give sweat and loyalty to a hope that reaches not only out to the outer limits of time's horizon, but beyond even that? The answer to such *why's* is in the confidence that God has spoken through

61

His Son, and that in Him fear and frustration find their Conqueror.

It takes the love of other persons to turn the Resurrection announcement into a piece of unbelievably good news. It takes enchantment with the world itself. It also takes the risk of faith that the future is in God's hands, that beyond where ships have ever sailed there awaits not an impersonal darkness, but Someone to be trusted.

"No," says the agnostic, "the verdict is not in."

"No," says the atheist, "there is no God to understand."

There is a community that believes there is a God, and that He has disclosed enough of Himself to enable men to walk through this valley of years with poise.

That, for the time being, is enough to send us into the streets carrying brightly-colored flags.

9

Our Angels Have Rotor Blades

So Balaam rose in the morning, and saddled his ass, and went with the princes of Moab. But God's anger was kindled because he went; and the angel of the Lord took his stand in the way as his adversary. Now he was riding on the ass, and his two servants were with him. And the ass saw the angel of the Lord standing in the road, with a drawn sword in his hand; and the ass turned aside out of the road, and went into the field; and Balaam struck the ass, to turn her into the road. Then the angel of the Lord stood in a narrow path between the vineyards, with a wall on either side (Numbers 22: 21-24 RSV).

* * * * * * * * * * * *

The San Bernardino Freeway looks good tonight. All traffic moving normally, except for a slight problem at Peck Road South where there's a car stalled in lane one, but the wrecker's getting him out of the way. Take your time, folks. It's been a good day; let's all get home safely. Um-m! Just got a whiff of someone's backyard barbecue. Back to control. This is Skywatch number four!

MOST LARGE CITIES now monitor rush hour traffic with helicopters. As they hover over the city, and as chopper pilots instruct motorists through car radios as to which routes are clearest and safest, with descriptions of the whole teeming ant colony from overhead, they bear an interesting resemblance to angels of the Bible.

Biblical angels are messengers of God who play opposite the demons. They bear heavenly instructions and furnish aid to men in trouble. Some of the best known stories concerning angels include a wrestling match at Bethel, an airborne choir announcing the birth of Jesus to shepherds watching their flocks by night, and a glistening agent who rescued Peter from prison. If we take the Bible seriously, we must take angels seriously. Still, how do such references make sense in an age of space? In a world filled with urgent questions and starved for moral leadership, who talks about angels?

How do we handle such references? Are we to treat them as part of a world view now altogether obsolete? How can we explain Michael, Gabriel, and an Angel of the Lord who with drawn sword obstructed Balaam's conscience-troubled path when he rode forth, at Balak's insistence, to pronounce a curse on Israel?

Angels are part of a mythological age which has, for most persons, drifted into intellectual obsolescence. They once served a purpose and enabled men to speak about God's presence in life's emergencies. Sometimes, the Presence meant sustenance and protection. Other times, it meant displeasure. Belief in a heavily populated unseen world was practically universal.

Until the sixteenth century men in general thought of space and time as though they were limited compartments in which objects were juxtaposed and interchangeable. They believed that a geometrical envelope could be traced round the totality of the stars. They talked, thinking they understood, of a first

63

and last moment discernible in the past and the future. They argued as though every element could be arbitrarily moved, without changing the world, to any point along the axis of time. The human mind believed itself to be perfectly at home in this universe, within which it tranquilly wove its patterns of metaphysics. And then one day, influenced by a variety of internal and external causes, this attitude began to change.

TEILHARD DE CHARDIN

The universe of early man was one occupied by realities more interesting than those indicated simply by pieces of rock or globes of gas orbiting on precision schedules. It was excitingly inhabited by life. It was an occupied universe. One had to call upon the help of the imagination, and rely upon poets and magicians to explain who all these beings were. Exact images were not the important thing. The important thing was that there was an invisible world as well as a visible one. All around men there was busyness and activity. God presided over the whole humming spectacle in sovereign splendor, but His love and help were as close as breathing. Angels bridged the mystery of how God could be so high above the life of man that to gaze upon Him would bring immediate death, and, at the same time, engage man on His level.

Angels are the product of the spiritual imagination, but they point to a truth so necessary to us that to discard them would be like ripping up earth's flowers and throwing them into the furnace. The purpose of poetry and theology (if there is a difference) is to trap aspects of feeling and sight which cannot otherwise be captured or identified. "I love you" is poetry. It is a set of vowels and consonants running after a miracle, yet never catching it. When men report having been addressed by angels, they have been trying to say that God has come close to them in their need, or in their shame. If such words or images do not satisfy us, at least men have tried to tell us what has happened to them in their journey through the world.

One way to relate angels to the modern mind is to describe them as fanciful superstition, to admit that they represent the elaborate mythology of the prescientific mind. Would that lead us toward, or away from, encounter with the transcendent? There is more tragedy than emancipation in the words of Israel Zangwill, written in 1900.

> The nymphs are gone, the fairies flown,
> The older presences unknown;
> The ancient gods forever fled.
> The stars are silent overhead,
> The music of the spheres is still.
> The later gods have followed Pan
> And man is left alone with man.

Here is the empty, deserted universe of the man who finds no reality at all except within the confined spaces of his own ego, where the courage to accept his abandoned condition is the mark of maturity. God having been written off as hoax, history having been adjudged without purpose or direction, life having been called inexplicable, a cruel joke, there is no need for angels. The razor's edge between being and nonbeing becomes bravery; the one ultimate enduring reality is death, death for everything, for everyone.

Faith attempts to build its explanations of reality upon certain premises, none of which is capable of proof, for they are either risked or rejected; the ultimate reality in life is God; God is good; God communicates this goodness to man and for man, as a sign of His own self-determined love.

The wonder of this thrusts us into the sky of poetry and a writing about angels, whether we like it or not. Angels are not the creatures of science. Science has no monopoly on the business of telling man who he is, what he was created to be, or even what his best possibilities are. Men of science reject that responsibility. Most men have high respect for the spiritual potential of humankind. Scientists do not speak of angels, but neither do they scoff. Instead, they would say, "That, my friend, belongs to the vocabulary of theology. It doesn't belong to the laboratory, but it may belong to the mystery of the soul."

Balaam knew, when the king of Moab first importuned him to

pronounce a curse upon Israel, that he would be wrong in doing it. He sent back word that not for all the money in Moab could he be persuaded to compromise his integrity and position; but the princes, whom the king of Moab sent, apparently spotted cracks in the will power of this respected prophet. When the emissaries came a second time, even though Balaam repeated his original refusal, he added, politically, that he would talk with God further. He then asked the Monarch's representatives to stay overnight. He said he would reassess his position and report later concerning his further consultations with God.

By the next morning, he was fully taken in by the attractive proposition, and the party set out. The story of how Balaam's donkey halted before an obstruction in the road and wouldn't proceed, how it turned out to be the angel of the Lord defying Balaam and asking him what he was doing going back on his commitment to speak the truth at all costs, is both humorous and prophetic. It may strike us as impossibly childish, but it makes its point. If we've never seen an angel standing in our way, while we were in the process of betraying our best self, it is because we wouldn't look. Balaam called it the angel of the Lord. We called it a guilty conscience. What did we mean by that?

While angels may no longer be intellectually credible, God, nevertheless, is profoundly present in the midst of life, and we still yearn for ways to be articulate about the reality of His influence. We want to understand, and we have a need to speak about how He meets us, challenges us, and upholds us in danger, disappointment and temptation.

Matthew says that when Jesus was in the desert ". . . angels came and ministered to him." It was an arid and lonely territory, but there were angels there. If you've found the secret of inner joy, you've had the help of angels. Possibly they weren't dressed like angels. Perhaps they wore a rough jacket, a handmade apron, or a green surgical gown in an emergency room, but they were divine agents. When they came to your rescue, you knew that they had been sent by the Father who remembers His children.

In the Revelation, there are a dozen references to angels. One is to an "angel standing in the sun." It is one of the Bible's ways of painting hope's own portrait. The writing comes out of the midst of persecution. It was born in the womb of danger, suckled at the breast of hardship. Revelation is a book about war. It is a tale of struggle between Light and Darkness. It is the most vivid poetry in the whole literature of man. It is language clothed in armor, girded for fighting. In the midst of extreme discouragement and defeat, the author recognizes "an angel standing in the sun."

Has life ever been like that? Things go from bad to worse. You can't recognize a way out. You go to bed with terror. You get up with tears. The air is full of futility. You despise the fact that you are alive. Then some unexpected kindness, a rift in the clouds, an undreamed of answer to a problem, a friendly hand, a loving word or a new possibility, and lo, an angel is standing there!

In the city, in Miami and Dayton, in places like Pittsburgh and settlements like Shreveport, God's ministry to human need takes many forms, and to speak of these ministries as the activities of God's angels is better than not to speak at all. The good news of the Christian faith is that the universe is not deserted. While the air is not split by angel wings, the morning and evening beat of rotor blades overhead speak of an encompassed and guarded life. "He will give his angels charge of you, and on their hands they will bear you up . . ." (Matthew 4:6 RSV).

The City is rich in ministries of healing. Here are the hospitals, the miracle-working specialists, the research laboratories, the clinics. Vast ministries of the mind are in the libraries, the lectures and the films. The ministries of Spirit are in the sounds of great orchestras, the sight of large ships moving out to sea, the parks, the botanical gardens, the museums and the Olvera streets. The ministry of work, the ministry of play, while some conserve and some expand, all are involved in the shaping of civilization's dream. Angels are everywhere. The role of the angel is that of the messenger. When we recognize by word and deed the message of God's care over us, we validate a belief in angels more convincingly than the entries, or lack of entries, in the logs of those who fly through space.

If Biblical angels bother you, and you don't quite know how to

67

explain to your children, try an experiment. Try the angel's vocation for a few days, and play the part of God's undercover agent. Begin looking for a way to help someone who needs help; then, when you've had a fling at that, try noticing angels around you, who are bringing happiness and encouragement, hope and health to your own moments of tiredness and despair. You'll believe in them all right; you won't be able to choose.

10

Nice People Go to the Races

The religious life of the churches has been a kind of make-believe in which a traditional piety and traditional forms of worship and preaching seemed to give security and sanction. In the moment of crisis, the gap between the world in which they were really living and the religious institution opened into a yawning chasm. The meaning of prayer, the character of death, the reality of sin and the truth of redemption somehow escaped them, even though they had given outward acknowledgement to the traditional piety. The profound guilt over broken relationships in work, perfidy in their personal history and adultery in their ideal marriages remained outside the preview of this piety. In the time of sickness, unemployment, or bereavement, these betrayals and prejudices flood in upon the person, revealing the emptiness of the traditional religious practice.

GIBSON WINTER

THERE WOULD be something incongruous about a picture of Jesus on a horse, yet horses were as much a part of the environment in Jesus' time as boats. We probably think of Jesus making most of his journeys on foot, because the Holy Land is small, and because the gospels make no mention of horses at all.

The Old Testament, though, abounds in references to them. The pounding of horses hooves and the dust and screech of chariot wheels run through all thirty-nine Books of the old Canon. The psalmist sang, "A war horse is a vain hope for victory." When Hezekiah, king of Jerusalem, was surrounded by a host of hostile Assyrian regiments, he tried to scare off the enemy by boasting that, in case of attack, he could count on the promise of many extra horses and chariots from Egypt. The Assyrian commander, on receiving the threat from outside the heavily guarded parapets, called up to the man in the tower, "Tell Hezekiah he's a fool. He's finished. Tell him he's putting his trust in the wrong places. What good are horses without men to ride them?"

In business, skills are more important than material resources, and in a church, people with commitment are more important than lounges. Let's try giving them a new name. Call them the thoroughbreds of humanity.

A thoroughbred is a horse with a history, a horse with spirit, a lean and swift animal, bred for racing. The renewal of society and of the church hang upon those same qualities. The call of Jesus is a call to be the spirited people of God.

Spirited, not spiritual—though the words are similar, there's a mile of meaning between them. Spiritual still may be a good word, but we have allowed it to become insipid, as if it described someone who lives on a diet of hymn books—someone who is good, but good for nothing in particular. I can think of no one who feels flattered by being called a spiritual person. On the other hand, I can think of no higher compliment to pay someone I admire than to say of him, "He is a great spirit."

Church leaders are reminded sometimes that their business is with spiritual realities and they ought to keep to their ecclesiastical knitting. This means, in the mind of the one who is trying to maintain this wall between the sacred and the secular, that one should speak about Jesus Christ and Moses, but not about the present. Speak about Paul and Timothy, but not about the gut

69

issues of human existence; speak about prayer and getting to heaven, but not about the world. Talk about how to discover private peace, but don't make anybody angry or upset. That kind of religion is already nine-tenths dead.

The word *spiritual* has some positive and useful meanings, and there is nothing wrong with a piety which says its prayers, studies the Bible, and thinks deeply about God. What does represent distortion is matching of the spirit of God with other than the blood-sweat-and-tears world we know so well. It is this world which is starving to be redeemed. It is this world of hardship and choice that the faith is about. We are promised that this isn't all, but we are fiercely reminded by our Leader that, for now, here is where the action is. "If a man say, I love God, and hateth his brother, he is a liar." It is hard to be blunter than that. "Inasmuch as ye have done it unto one of the least of these my brethren, ye have done it unto me."

The gospel does not announce that all men have become sinners, and that they must turn away from earthly to heavenly things. It affirms, that the church is called to be the dwelling place of God's spirit, and that it, in turn, calls men to live in the world and rejoice in it as men of spirit—as thoroughbreds whose curving Lexington muscles ripple with life, whose nostrils are filled with the smell of victory.

The thoroughbred spirit has two principal avenues of expression.

One is through the person, the other is through the church; for without the Spirit, the Christian church is about as important to the future of man as a marathon bingo game.

What difference does the Spirit make? How do we recognize His presence?

First, He creates the Christian. He creates the church, too, but first, the man—the man who cannot be measured by himself, but only by the yardstick of God.

He begins to create him, as Ezekiel put it, by first cleansing his life. "I will sprinkle clean water upon you, and you shall be clean from all your uncleannesses, and from all your idols. . . ." Then, the prophet adds, on God's behalf, "A new heart I will give you, and a new spirit I will put within you; and I will take out of your flesh the heart of stone and give you a heart of flesh."

The spirit of God makes man a spirit, and saves him from being a rock.

Another thing that happens to him, is that he discovers a sense of wholeness about his existence. The connection between the word *Holy* (as in Holy Spirit) and *whole* or *wholeness* is not accidental. Holiness is wholeness, the opposite of splitness.

Goethe said, "Two souls, alas! reside within my breast." He was lucky. Most people feel more in common with another man who confessed

> Within my earthly temple there's a crowd;
> There's one of us that's humble, one that's proud,
> There's one that's broken-hearted for his sins,
> There's one that unrepentant sits and grins;
> There's one that loves his neighbor as himself,
> And one that cares for naught but fame and pelf;
> From much corroding care I could be free
> If I could once determine which is me.
>
> EDWARD SANFORD MARTIN

The thoroughbred Spirit is the spirit of Jesus of Nazareth re-created in us. Theological books dance all around the problem as to the exactness of identity between the Holy Spirit and the Spirit of Jesus, but the answer always comes out about the same. All we really understand about the Holy Spirit, we understand in terms of the Christ Spirit. To become the friend of Jesus is to become the friend of the Holy Spirit, and is to find the key to life in His spirit. Paul described the "fruits of the spirit" as love, joy, peace, patience, kindness, goodness, trustfulness, gentleness and self-control, and it is obvious that these were all adjectives taken directly from the Galilean.

We are called to live in and by it. To live the spirited, rather than the spiritual, life is to discover ourselves, for man is spirit—God's breath! Jesus, as incarnate Spirit, becomes God's kiss upon

71

man's lips. When Adlai Stevenson fell dead from a heart attack on a London Street, Marietta Trees tried to revive the fallen statesman by mouth-to-mouth resuscitation. London newspapers, in reporting the life-saving effort, called it the attempted kiss of life. I had not heard that expression before. It's a stunning phrase, and it could refer to another great statement from Genesis—how God breathed upon man and he became a living soul.

The church, too, drinks its life from the Spirit of God.

The Holy Spirit in the church is the spirit of action, movement, reform, mission and ministry. Its spirit is not something contained in a strong box, nor is it confined by the sacraments. These are simply arrows which point to the Spirit at work. The big word now, so far as the church is concerned, is renewal. God apparently is saying to the church, "Renew yourself or die."

The history of huge prehistoric animals which once roamed the continent, including large elephants in our American Southwest, has a lesson about our ability, or inability, to adjust to change. Some refuse to change. They go down fighting with gritted teeth and rigid backs. Still, change is a law of life no man can break. He who fights the future has a dangerous enemy.

Not all change is good. It cannot be denied that the Spirit is leading the church onto new ground and into new forms of ecumenical expression. Things are not the same. Sometimes that flow creates within us a nostalgia and feeling of discouragement. Most congregations now are fighting to stay statistically even. Most churchmen feel that they are swimming against a tide. If the church worries more about the danger of losing its nerve than its members, it not only will survive, it will prevail.

In the same way, the Spirit calls men to personal wholeness, He also calls the church to ecumenical completeness. A Christian's vocation is to represent the good news of God to other men, not protect a denominational interest. Some will try to fulfill these objectives through a Presbyterian form of government; others within the evangelical tradition known as the Methodist Church, still others as Roman Catholics, but all are under obligation to be Christians first. The Consultation on Church Union is a story about wholeness. It is not a mechanical tinkering, nor power play to keep Catholics from scoring an end run. It is the church exploring itself, praying for a wider unity, attempting to take seriously the prayer of Jesus that all might be one.

The search for community is a search that will never end. We cannot be men alone. There is haughtiness and blindness in thinking we could be. Aware of the illusion of any private hot line to God, and the inappropriateness of a purely individualized witness to God in mass society, we unite in congregations; we organize as districts and presbyteries; we come together in councils.

It is important to be a conscientious human being, but it is not enough to be just that. Politically, it is important to vote, but people must do more than that. They must contribute to parties, write letters, attend meetings, sign petitions and join strength with others, who hope to see the same things accomplished. The church is no different. The spirit of the church is no benevolent smog, floating in the air. It is God working through congregations, votes, and pocketbooks.

The Holy Spirit works beyond as well as within the institution. Today He is clearly striving within and through a wide and mysterious fellowship of Protestant, Catholic and Orthodox Christians, humbly spoken of as the people of God.

Christians have a thoroughbred's history. We carry the silks of kings. We were baptized at a starting gate and trained by men who believed we should lay aside every weight and the sin which so easily besets us, and run the race that is ours, looking to Jesus the Author and Pioneer of our faith.

We are people, not horses, but there is a thoroughbred quality in our blood—faith's chromosomes and flame!

> Spirit of the living God,
> Fall a-fresh on me.
> Spirit of the living God,
> Fall a-fresh on me.
> Break me, melt me, mold me, fill me;
> Spirit of the living God
> Fall a-fresh on me.
>
> DANIEL IVERSON

11

Strange Things Happen in Motel Rooms

Be watchful, stand firm in your faith, be courageous, be strong

(I Corinthians 16:13 RSV).

THE TELEPHONE RANG and a man's well-modulated voice on the other end asked for an appointment as soon as possible.

"I'm at the Franklin House. I'd like to come right over. It's urgent."

Franklin House is an expensive motel in the Valley. The clock on the study wall showed five minutes till four. It was October. I remembered I was under instructions to pick up a head of lettuce at the store on the way home. We were having guests.

"I'll be happy to talk with you. The church is on the south side of Wilshire, five or six blocks east of the San Diego Freeway. You should make it here in fifteen minutes."

Fifteen minutes later, he was telling me his name.

"Joe—Joe Rayburn from Fresno. Joseph Rayburn, alcoholic, University of California graduate, president of Sigma Chi, successful salesman, father of three beautiful kids, member and director of the Bayville Country Club and member of the Presbyterian Church. But a lousy—pardon me—son-of-a-gun who, until this morning, has not been really sober since he left home on this trip seven days ago—really sloppy Joe! The ax fell this morning."

"What do you mean, the ax fell?" I asked. The lowering sun struck the large blue stone in the fraternity ring on his left hand, in an explosion of light. He was dressed sharply. His eyes were serious.

There was a long silence. My training warned me against breaking it. There we sat looking at each other. I heard the secretary leave and knew it must be four-thirty. Head of lettuce . . . get home on time. "The ax fell." What was back of that remark? I saw his throat tighten, then relax. I offered him a cigarette.

74

He stood up, took a couple of steps over to a chair and with one foot up, and his back partly to me, said, "Early this morning something happened to me, and I'm still shaking. I take it you believe in God?"

"Correct. I believe in God."

Silence again. I got up from the desk and walked over and stood near him. Outside, the traffic was beginning to get heavy. The room was alive with uncountable arrows of slanting sunlight. I was trying to help him get it out.

Suddenly, he faced me square on, and bit into the thing that was pressing on his mind. "This morning while I was lying in my bed, God spoke to me."

"What did God say?"

He waited a long time before replying. He was filled with doubt as to whether I, or anyone, would take him seriously, but he had to get it out. He had to.

Looking me squarely in the eyes, he answered the question.

"He said, 'Joe, get out of that bed, stand up: be a man!'" He repeated the command, as if he scarcely could believe it himself. "Get out of that bed: stand up: be a man." Then, he told me, the turning point in his life had come. With God's help, he would make a new beginning.

We talked for a time and finally went for a cup of coffee together. Later, we walked to his car and shook hands.

"Good luck," I said. "I think you'll make it."

I went into the deserted nave and sat alone for a long time. Light reaching low through the stained glass dappled the pews with color. I pondered the whole business of how God gets through to human beings—how, sometimes, it's like pinpoint bombing as God touches a man's soul with precisely the right word. "Get out of that bed, Joe; stand up: be a man."

I wandered back into the study, prepared to go home. Before locking my desk, I picked up a New Testament lying there and thumbed through the Letters. Suddenly my eyes locked onto a sentence:

"Be watchful, stand firm in your faith . . . be strong."

Get out of that bed, Joe. That is where solutions begin, with sloughing off the shackles of self-pity and beginning to act in

75

affirmative ways. That's what God did. He moved. He did something. We will not always do the right thing; most of the time we will. James writes, "[Be] doers of the word. . . ." The call to Christian obedience is not a call to sit back and watch Him take over the solution of our problems.

We worry. We try one route, then another. We toss and turn, agonize and fret, speculate, fulminate, but often we do not act.

A few avoid the hand wringing. They go to work. When emergencies arise, they put a pie in the oven, start for their tools or hit the telephone. I envy them. Too often, I mull over right versus wrong ways to proceed. In the meantime, someone else has stepped forward into the vacuum of the need. "Joe, get out of that bed. You won't find the answer there staring at the ceiling. Get out of the jail into which you've locked yourself!" Where is the man who hasn't, at some time, died temporarily, whose power hasn't failed, whose engines haven't flamed out high over the city of his dreams? Where is the man or woman who hasn't had the need to hear these words, "Be strong. You can do it! Get in there and fight the way you've been taught to fight. You're a Christian, remember, a baptized Christian, and here you are, lying on your back as if all these years of God-talk were myths. Pick yourself up, dust yourself off, and start all over again."

This isn't the center of the gospel, but it reminds us that a man is capable of acting or responding to circumstances once he's heard the gospel, if he's spent even a short while gazing on the cross God used to divide history in two. It is not, in itself, the good news that once set the world on its ear, but it can be good news to a man whose spirit is tired and who has lost the will to try.

To the Christian, what these words mean is this: because God is strong, you can be strong. Because Christ is risen, there are no circumstances in which victory is not possible. Because the Father still sends His Spirit into the hearts of men, the admonition to be strong is more than a slap on the back, more than a rosy optimism offering escape into a world of make-believe. It is the artificial respiration of the Holy Spirit, blown within to restart the engines of confidence—confidence that this remains God's world, that we are His children, and that His concern and love are close at hand.

A Colorado jurist made news across the country a few years back when, from his juvenile court bench, he issued an ultimatum to youngsters who said they got into trouble because there just wasn't anything for them to do. Judge Harold Gillian gave them the following advice.

Nothing to do? Then go home. Clean out the garage. Mow the yard. Help put up the storm windows. Offer your assistance to the County Recreation Department. Take some flowers to someone who is ill. Build something with your hands. Write a letter. Help your minister. Fix anything that is broken. Do something that will improve your neighborhood. Help your school, assist your parents, better your country. Join a club, learn a language or to play a musical instrument. Get interested in birds or astronomy. Find a part-time job, tutor someone younger than yourself, go out for athletics, and if, in the evening you're not too tired, read a book. Stop acting as if the world owed you happiness. Start living as if there were only half enough time to do all the things that are worth doing and that need to be done.

Get out of bed, Joe. Stand up. There seems to be a clear coherence between what Joe said he heard God saying to him, and Paul's advice to the Corinthians, "Be watchful, stand firm in your faith. . . ." Paul was warning against a falling away from the truths about Jesus Christ he had taught them some months before. Writing from Ephesus, he rallies them on, urging steadfastness in the Christian life. *Stand* is one of his greatest words. Take up God's armor, then you will be able to stand your ground when things are at their worst, and to complete every task and still to stand. Stand firm, I say, stand!

To stand is to stay with something in which you believe. To stand up is to cast your vote for it. Standing can be hard in an age of conformity. Bishop Gerald Kennedy tells how a student stole examination questions and had them mimeographed, on the campus of a midwestern state university. Having subscribed to our present-day success philosophy in full, he sold them for five-dollar a copy. They were circulated among various groups living on the campus. According to the dean, though many knew, no one reported this to the administration; only one student stood out against it. He refused to have anything to do with it, whereupon most of them regarded him with less than friendly eyes. When the scandal broke, and the student body began to realize what was involved, this student emerged as something of a hero. Commented the dean to Kennedy, "We're a little shy of heroes."

Our ultimate business is with God, and God's business with us is stated in the Son. Stand firm in that faith. Stand for it. Stand with it, and you can stand up to the worst life can throw at you.

Southern California has an abundance of kooks. That word means that we have found people who are not like ourselves, and it disturbs the waters of the glassy pond into which we are staring. The word could mean something else, too. It could mean manhood distorted by pointless experimentation. Jesus is our reference. His life creates for us the possibility of being what Joe wanted to be— a man!

A real man the church likes to remember is Maltbie Babcock. Along with his own personhood, he also had a poetic sensitivity which produced the hymn "This is My Father's World." Another song he taught the church would interest Joe.

> Be strong! We are not here to play, to dream, to drift:
> We have hard work to do and loads to lift;
> Shun not the struggle: face it,
> 'Tis God's gift.
>
> Be strong! Say not the days are evil—
> Who's to blame? And fold the hands and acquiesce—
> O shame! Stand up, speak out, and bravely
> In God's Name.
>
> Be strong! It matters not how deep entrenched the wrong,
> How hard the battle goes, the day, how long;
> Faint not, fight on!
> Tomorrow comes the song.

12

Several Things Besides Air Need Clearing Up

It is too late to go back to the small city, and I don't see any
reason why we should go back to it. . . . I am interested in
the values that this city represented, and not in the city itself.

CONSTANTINOS A. DOXIADIS

SMOG HAS REACHED all the way to Hawaii. For a long time, Los
Angeles was believed to have a monopoly on the dirty yellow cloud;
then Wilmington admitted it, too, had it—then New York, Cleveland, St. Louis, Denver and now Honolulu.

Smog is a diffused non-security blanket of noxious fumes. It
obscures the skyline, turns eyes red and sets up yearnings for the
farm. There are as many theories about its source and eradication
as there have been *Hello Dolly!* performances by Carol Channing.
One suggestion, on the West Coast, has been to drill holes through
the mountains. Using gigantic fans, it is proposed to blow the city's
bad breath out onto the desert. Other speculative solutions are to
substitute electric batteries for combustion engines in automobiles,
to put factories underground, to call up the Rand Corporation, or
to move to Australia.

Air pollution is a growing problem like nuclear death, but
without the red telephones or loud noises, just slow respiratory
poisoning.

Along with the wide screens, surfboards and "I Left My Heart
in San Francisco," smog is another of California's gifts to the
nation. At least, California had the name first.

It is an ugly word for an ugly fact. A blend of smoke, dust and
industrial vapors, it is an inescapable part of city life.

There are several things besides air that need clearing up. Smog
is not only a pollutant: it is also the perfect symbol for an age

79

characterized by smoke and fog, by ambiguity, vagueness and obscured solutions.

What, for example, has been more muddied than the matter of what represents a responsible role for the United States in Asia? Where is the narrow band of reason, within which law and order is neither a hieroglyph for repressing and defending the status quo, nor a mouthed cliché—as if no awful price had been paid for constitutional government? The new morality, rightly understood, is a step toward love and away from legalism as the controlling criteria of conduct, but the atmosphere of personal decision remains miserably murky.

Cities have the same problems: how to meet the need for more schools, streets, libraries, and jails; how to reform antiquated, village-style governments; where to get revenue, where to find enough water and parking spaces. These are the perennial ones, expressed in the task of feeding, clothing, housing, healing, and entertaining millions of people at one time in one location.

The crisis list is shorter, tougher, meaner. It includes volatile words like police, poverty and prejudice.

These are human, not mechanical, dilemmas. To them, the community of faith has something to say, something about freedom, something about persons, something about reconciliation and love.

Police always stand in between order and disorder, between those who have power and those who are trying to gain it. Though they are under obligation to protect all citizens, they are, by the nature of things, identified with the *ins*. In America, this has meant whites. Police hating by browns and blacks is not too hard to understand. It is second nature for the man in Hough to look upon the police as the white man's mercenaries, even before he has fastened his tie, or pinned on his badge. The policeman does not live there, if he can help it, and the least show of authority is met with cries of brutality.

Police now are deserting their cruisers and even walking the beat in blazers, where their sincerity and good intentions will show. Police-community relations continue to baffle most heads of urban governments. The policeman is the key to a frustrated urban America. He alone can enable the city to buy the time it must have to relieve the human pressures of deteriorating neighborhoods, soaring

80

crime, bad schools, the coalescing hostility of the black and the poor.

We can only expect the policeman's help if there is increased understanding of his role from all sides. The Establishment must realize why the man who lives on Grape Street feels the way he does, and practice projecting its own desire for dignity and respect onto the person who is often dealt with as a potential malefactor first, and as a man, second. The man in the position of disadvantage must disinfect himself from the belief that the policeman is the enemy, or that he has sold his soul to the company store. The man in the ghetto who demands respect must also grant it, or be responsible for losing his own case. Police have the toughest job of all. They must understand both duty and dreams. They must not set themselves against either side. They must reverence the American idea that sovereignty is in the people as a whole and teach themselves to stay sensitive and humane in the face of evidence that there is hardly any form of barbarism that they will not have to look at daily in some of their fellow men.

Christian faith is concerned both with order and with justice. Order, because God has given order to the universe itself and there is no freedom for anyone without it, and justice because God is just, and justice is the crucial implementation and proof of worship. Theologian Reinhold Niebuhr has said that if these two qualities of existence must be ranked, order comes first, though it is a most reluctant concession.

Stephen Becker, in a novel called *A Covenant With Death,* argues that tyranny is more to be feared than anarchy.

Comments Judge Lewis in a legal opinion in the closing part of the book, "In a stable society anarchy, though often conspicuous, tends to be self-limiting; tyranny, though often inconspicuous, tends to be self-aggravating."

Freedom rides a razor's edge.

Welfare is another staggering dimension of urban existence with thousands of families now into the third generation having depended upon the check all their lives. There was a time when it was generally assumed that large numbers of persons on welfare were in that situation out of sheer laziness and irresponsibility.

Charges of deliberately bearing children outside of marriage to increase Aid to Dependent Children, welfare cheating, and refusing to accept jobs even when offered, made a neat package of blame.

American leadership now recognizes that the problem isn't that simple. A system which throws any kind of regularly guaranteed income into jeopardy as the result of accepting a day-and-a-half's labor worth $16.50, and which brings down the wrath of society upon the man who isn't willing to risk it, must be mistaken and has to be changed.

Welfarism cannot be isolated from its associated diseases: ignorance, rotten teeth, brittle bones and poverty of spirit. Welfare policies are presently up for radical review and guaranteed minimum incomes are almost a reality. A new age is here. We are already into it with fantastic new capacities for meeting human needs. There is a new set of frontiers, and one is the legitimacy, wisdom and economy involved in assuring everyone of enough money to live in safety and dignity.

The gospel contends all men live by the grace of God. It doesn't differentiate between the man who defrauds the state by a crooked income tax return and the woman who uses welfare funds to buy beer. What it does insist upon is that every human being bears the stamp of God and that whenever one person treats another like livestock, or a toy, that person sins, violating the world and adding to the problem of smog.

Prejudice is a word that has gone into the attic along with *brotherhood* and *progress*. Those words were too tame, too lacking in bite. They perished with the Edsel and the homecoming parade. They were replaced by a new militancy and now-ism. While there are things to be said on both sides of evolution versus revolution, no purpose is served by lamenting a choice history has already made. Revolution it is. If I were black, I wouldn't be willing to wait, either.

But *prejudice* still helps illuminate the issue. We cannot build a society or civilization, or even a life of our own, without judgment. Judgment and choice are at the heart of our humanness. An ability to make judgments gets near to whatever it is that is divine about us. God does not call us to be men of distinction, but men who

82

make distinctions—between what is true or false, greedy or generous. Where we disobey God is not by judging, but by using improper criteria, or by denying a person the chance to validate himself—by prejudging him, slamming the door in his face.

The United Presbyterian Church made a try at cleaning up the air men breathe by including in its 1967 confessional statement the following statement of principles.

> God has created the peoples of the earth to be one universal family. In his reconciling love he overcomes the barriers between brothers and breaks down every form of discrimination based on racial or ethnic difference, real or imaginary. The Church is called to bring all men to receive and uphold one another as persons in all relationships of life, in employment, housing, education, leisure, marriage, family, church, and the exercise of political rights. Therefore the church labors for the abolition of all racial discrimination and ministers to those injured by it. Congregations, individuals, or groups of Christians who exclude, dominate, or patronize their fellow men, however subtly, resist the Spirit of God and bring contempt on the faith which they profess.

God is spirit. The word for spirit in the New Testament is *pneuma*, air. His spirit has power to cut through the putrid haze which now has enveloped most of the cities in which men live and where they are determined to stay.

Also capable of penetration is a song. One, urban man might well learn to sing, is to the tune of "Go Tell It On The Mountain."

Go tell it in the city,
Shout from the housetops
Everywhere!
Go tell it in the city,
That Jesus Christ is Lord.

Sing praises for the city,
Its color, pulse and din,
The buildings shooting skyward:
The city's made of men.

Sing praises for the city,
Its rhythm beats the air;
The factories, stores and traffic
All speak that man is there.

Sing praises for the city,
Its failures, guilt and sin;
With all its cold indifference,
Still the city's made of men.

Sing praises for the city,
Its sprawling urban span;
Its constant changing patterns
Reflect the face of man.

Sing praises for the city,
And tell all men the word:
That man who makes the city
Is made of Christ the Lord.

Now, try a big, deep breath!

III
BE SURE TO TALK TO STRANGERS

13

That's God Over the Fireplace

Very specific definitions are in order. Who *is* God? Do we feel
God is a man, a woman, white, black, American, a busy
heavenly switchboard operator, love, Charlton Heston-in-the-
sky, an angry, hating monster who runs torture chambers, a
kind elderly bishop with a beard, or what? In my own experience, God is the spirit of loving instead of murder, of
relationship rather than fragmentation.

MALCOLM BOYD

GOD HAS SURVIVED the rumor that He is dead; still things aren't
the same as they were.

Let's hear it for the God-is-Dead boys. They did us a favor.
They really rattled the chandeliers. They forced the church out
into the light. They raised hell with every tradition in the book.
They frightened the pants off us, but they also were responsible
for a lot of spiritual growing up.

Many of us still believe in God—a God who is more than a
tender memory, more than a treasured oil suspended over the
fireplace of a grandfather who gave us nickels when we were
little.

We are more careful now about what we allow the word *God*
to mean. Standing alone, it means everything—and nothing.
Standing alone, it is a pagan word, a nude syllable, a word used
by one man to describe a monstrous autocrat stalking the sky, by
another to define a pervasive, renewing Spirit, working silently,
invisibly, but with irresistible force and significance in the lives
of men.

One of the chief difficulties connected with faith is that of trying to think about God, to find a place to stand while we work away at the questions, "Who am I? What am I doing here?"

Most of us have grown up thinking of God in personal terms. We mix trees, waterfalls and sky in, too. God is more like a shepherd than a sunset, more like a man than a mountain.

Urban man has not abandoned his faith in God altogether, but his ideas of God are so vague and devoid of meaning that they play no more part in the regulation of his life than the benevolent memory of the ancestor whose portrait hangs over the fireplace in the library.

Rural man's world was one of soil and seasons, of work with his hands, of daily contact with life and death. He drew his water from the well, ruled with firmness over the affairs of his family and rested on Sunday. Somehow, the wisdom of God was back of all events.

Urban man lives in a world of machines, money and media. He is insulated from the earth by concrete, and from all sorts of immediate experiences through the buying of services and a religion of privacy. He is not dependent upon the weather, nor upon his neighbor, nor upon the faith. He doesn't wonder about his destiny; he manufactures it.

At the same time, he has questions about the validity and the worthwhileness of his set up. Something seems to be missing. Creature comforts are not enough to satisfy him. His life lacks dimension, love and hope. The Big Man in the sky is too small a god to depend upon or relate to. Where to go from there? Abstract reasoning leaves him cold, and talk that God is real seems like monstrous arrogance.

A new world is emerging, a new age, a new kind of society and man. Traditional concepts of God are increasingly useless, but the reality they point to is beyond the power of destruction. Urban man can no longer write and think primarily in terms of the God of meadows, quietness, and one-to-one fulfilment and the commandments. Life is irrevocably corporate and mechanized; it is swift, noisy and headed wildly out into space. Life is instant food, the ghetto, the commuter flight, credit cards, and someplace to go; but God is at home in the city, too, and, in an expanded universe,

His invitation to men to live lives of joy and peace, of holiness and compassion, of faith and responsibility remains unchanged.

Recognizing the peril of idolatry, Christians nevertheless form an image of God in their minds out of their knowledge of Jesus. At the same time, they keep reminding themselves that God is Spirit, not Superman, not Super-Jesus. Is this a valid way to think and speak about God in the space age?

The Bible gives no clear picture of God. It spans around two thousand years of time and, across that spectrum, even inspired men's ideas of how best to articulate God's nature and presence have varied. In the earliest Old Testament writings, God is thought of as a powerful Being who is the greatest among all the inhabitants of heaven. He has quasi-human form. Moses, in one place, refers to Him as "The Lord [who] spoke with you face to face at the mountain, out of the midst of the fire." According to the prophets, He becomes the only God. While Isaiah speaks of God as the One who "sits above the circle of the earth," the prophets speak of Him as the God of Spirit whose main manifestations in the world are justice and love and peace. In the New Testament, with the coming of Jesus into human experience, there is a healthy clarification which appears in this sentence, "No one has ever seen God; [but] the only Son, who is in the bosom of the Father, he has made him known" (John 1:18).

This adds up to the fact that God is above human thought. The best man is capable of is recognizing, in his experience, glimpses of the Divine nature, and of seeing here and there intimations of God's presence; then of using the most exalted and meaningful forms of speech available to him to describe the Indescribable.

We call God "our Father." This is an image. It is a partial image, a picture taken out of the scrapbook of our own finite existence, and it helps.

I loved my own father very much. He meant many things to me. To call God "Father" is to bring me a little nearer in understanding who God is and what He is like. We call God Creator, and again we are borrowing from life. What does it mean to create something? It means to build a building, paint a picture, write a book. We know what the experience of creation is. We know that out of formlessness can come form; out of unrelated elements, relationships and beauty can emerge. And the theatre! Ah, there creation runs wild, and the spirit of man in music, dance and imagination furnish countless clues to God, the Creator of all. We say God is love, for we know what it means to love and be loved, so we exclaim, "God is like this!" God is not blind fear, nor vindictiveness, nor uncaringness, nor amorality. God is love, and God is like love. What love is, God is. When Jesus was born and lived, suffered and died, and then by a miracle which words fail to explain, withstood or overcame death's power, men said—history said—looking at Jesus, "God is like *this*. We have seen God in flesh! *This* is God in all His earthly fullness."

Jesus, the church likes to say, is God's self-disclosure, God's revelation of Himself to the world. It is God meeting man on the level of his own life and his own history, and thus communication *with* man, and *to* man, is the stern and glorious meaning of his life.

Where does God as a person come in? Is it because Jesus is a person that through this perfect identification with God we begin to speak of God as a person? No. In Christian thought, we do not say God is a person, but that God is personal. At least, that's what we mean. Remember, we are in the business of describing the Indescribable, of trying to express in finite terms that which is not finite. Because human personality is a kind of supreme form of existence, and because personality is, in fact, the highest, the holiest, the greatest, the most dynamic, the most beautiful, the most meaningful thing we know, we use the language of personality to speak of God. Nothing in or about the space age invalidates, nor is likely to invalidate, truth of that order.

God is not a man. He is spirit; but what is Spirit? It's something we know exists, something that's real, yet our eyes cannot see nor our hands touch Spirit; so, we invent the word *spirit* to help us out of a dilemma. The word *person* is the shining, indispensable word we bring to bear upon our desire to speak of God, for to be a person is to be something rare and significant and precious amidst all the panoramic wonders of existence.

To speak of God as personal is not to dwarf God, nor turn him into a kind of cosmic giant. It is not, to use J. B. Phillips' expression, to settle for a God who is too small for the immensities of the stars. It is rather to make God great, and to use the ultimate image available to us to speak of Him, who is both Source and Goal of all our living.

To be a person is not to be a body, a hundred and fifty pounds of flesh with eyes and fingers and teeth. A deeper meaning of personhood is the power to love, the power to choose and the ability to participate meaningfully in destiny. This begins to get down to what we mean by using the language of persons and the attributes of personality in our conversation about God. We use the language of personality and speak in personal terms because we want to say that we are related to God as a *Thou* rather than as an *It*. We are not related to God as we are to a mathematical equation or to the Pacific Ocean, but as to a friend or to a lover. We are not loved by propositions but by persons. Our prayers do not begin with "O Divine Principle" or "O Hallowed Essence of Truth," or "Hey You!" but with "Our Father, who art in heaven."

Heaven is picture-book language. We do not know anything about heaven. All we know (and this we only know by faith) is that the love of God can be trusted beyond the hour of our death, and that there is something to look forward to beyond this life. Both the intuition of our hearts and the assurances of Jesus persuade us this is so.

The space age is not an embarrassment to Biblical faith nor to our belief in the God to whom the Scriptures bear experiential witness. At times, we may have a kind of sneaking suspicion that it is, and that science, on many fronts, is carrying us into a realm that will wind up making the Bible's view of man and God and Creation and history obsolete. Perhaps this is so because the Bible does give us the impression that the earth and its people are God's main (perhaps even exclusive) interest, that earth is the center of the created order, that the sun is in the sky because earth needs its warmth and light, that man is God's highest form of workmanship and that all else in the universe is subordinate to man. Now we're not at all sure that this is a presupposition we have a right to make. As scientific horizons have expanded, our views about the centralism of man and earth have diminished.

91

Along with new cosmic perspective, there have come other revolutions in human thought, theology included. We read the Bible in a different way from our grandparents. Dietrich Bonhoeffer has given us a phrase which calls attention to this profound change in viewpoint. The world, he says, has come of age. Man is twenty-one, now, and his views of God and himself ought to be, and are, more mature than they were when man thought of God as a figure in the sky who sent the floods, stalked the heavens when His children were bad, and regulated human affairs through an infinitely complex, but unchangeable, celestial switchboard. Which is not to say that the Bible has been discredited, but that it must be read today in the context of the intellectual and historical times out of which it came.

One day at a wedding reception, I fell into conversation with a stranger. Soon after her discovery that I was a clergyman she said, with a bit of good-natured twinkle in her eye, "How do you know there is a God?"

"I don't," I said, and that really stopped her for a moment. She was used to professors of religion posing as people with all the answers. "I don't know there is a God the way that I know there is a city called Forth Worth, Texas, having been there and seen it. I believe in God as a matter of faith. If I knew beyond any doubt that God exists, and that He is interested in me, even adores me, I wouldn't need the word *faith*. I simply could align myself with a new block of information. I choose to live by faith that God is, and that He is *He*, not *it*, and that He's not Someone to take lightly. He's really quite important in everything I think and do and feel and want to become."

The space age does not tear down such faith. It only makes it more credible and necessary. Space probes, even genetics, with all the new data they furnish, are not going to eradicate the values of trust, responsibility, goodness and love. These values and realities are the true imperishables and are as indestructible as anything can be, because they are grounded in eternity. They flow from God and they give us the vocabulary with which to speak about God. It is easy to argue that man created God to satisfy his emotional hunger and need for security, and you may wish to believe that. Good luck if you do. Christianity puts it the other way around;

92

while God didn't really need man, He did covet man's fellowship and man's love, freely returned, and the flow is in that direction. *The New York Times* once carried this editorial.

The creature who descended from a tree or crawled out of a cave is now on the eve of incredible journeys. Yet it is not these journeys which chiefly matter. Will we be happier, wiser or better for seeing the other side of the moon or strolling in the meadows of Mars? The greatest adventure of all is not to explore the rings of Saturn. It is rather to try to understand the heart and soul of man, to adventure in turning away from wrath and destruction toward creativeness and love.

Is it not to discover what the gospel means when it speaks? Only the rich, warm, and sublime language of persons will suffice to present the Word of God.

14

Every City Needs a Tree

She looked down into the yard. The tree whose leaf umbrellas had curled around, under and over her fire escape had been cut down because the housewives complained that wash on the lines got entangled in its branches. The landlord had sent two men and they had chopped it down.

But the tree hadn't died . . . it hadn't died.

A new tree had grown from the stump and its trunk had grown along the ground until it reached a place where there were no wash lines above it. Then it had started to grow towards the sky again.

Annie, the fir tree, that the Nolans had cherished with waterings and manurings, had long since sickened and died. But

this tree in the yard—this tree that men chopped down . . .
this tree that they built a bonfire around, trying to burn up
its stump—this tree lived!

It lived! And nothing could destroy it.

BETTY SMITH

A CITY cannot be all cement. If it is, men will die. Even one tree
can redeem a brick and neon wilderness, whether it grows in
Brooklyn or near the spot where you wait each morning for the
Sixth Avenue Express.

Trees are useful also for nests, for producing lumber and for
providing shelter. Californians enjoy their state's massive redwoods;
Michigan has huge forests of pine and oak—New England, maple
and elm.

Children like to climb trees, and when they become adults, they
still like to get up high where they can see great distances, and
get better perspectives. They enjoy eating in penthouse restaurants
or looking over sparkling carpets of lights from edge-of-the-city
hilltops.

If you've toured Florida, you may have taken time to ride to the
top of the Citrus Tower where you can look out over eight million
orange trees. Perhaps, like me, you never cease to enjoy looking
down on rooftops from the window of a plane.

A Dali painting has the viewer looking down upon the cross of
Christ from high above it. That's where we are now, above the cross,
looking down upon the nailed hands, and the soldiers shooting
craps. We look past it, also, to a world busy with planting fields,
knocking down old buildings and putting up new ones, designing
anti-missile systems, filling out tax forms, and getting supper. But
what does the site of the murder of Jesus have to do with this?

Calvin Miller, in his book *Once Upon a Tree*, imagines the impact the Crucifixion would be apt to have if it had happened yesterday. He begins with a press release from United Press International.

The United Arab Republic announced by repeated broadcast
on Radio Cairo, that Jesus Bar Joseph was executed for

inciting riots and aiding in insurrection. His repeated inferences that he was some sort of king or leader seemed to be a threat to the national and international stability of many Near Eastern countries. His execution seemed unprotested even by his closest followers. Officials in Tel Aviv felt that Jesus, who only days earlier had caused a riot in Jerusalem, might be planning a military coup. Although no specific charge has, as yet, been released concerning his execution, it is generally known that he was openly unsympathetic with the present political regime of that country.

. . . This dispatch would probably have been followed by half-a-dozen other reports of world trouble spots. All the smart new words in the glossary of political science would be used— *unilateral, junta, cease fire, aggressor, disarmament, provocative, imperialist.* This would be followed by local news, weather, and sports. Then, after a sandwich and a glass of milk, Mr. America and his family turn off the TV and go to bed.

He isn't the first author to try to relocate that event in modern times, but his way of putting it sounds uncommonly accurate. It's about the way it would come off.

By a mystery, though, the cross's meaning and authority within the human situation has not been quickly dismissed, even though it had as much competition for men's attention in Herod's age as it would today. The racket and roar of empire, the marching feet of combatant forces, the thirst for excitement and pleasure and the static of competing philosophies and theologies merged to muffle the cross then, as well. The Christ's cross was only one of three, but it changed, and still is changing the world.

From our imaginary perch, the world and our prospects within it look like this.

First, it is a split world—a fragmented, divided thing in search of wholeness and reunion.

Second, it is a world unable by its own cleverness and will to save itself.

Third, it is a world which holds in rough and blistered hands a gospel—a small handful of cloud. What it means is that because

95

God reigns, because God cares, because He is involved, there is reason to live a life of optimism and hope. This may be using too much language to say something very simple. Love has entered the flow of history; the principal mark of this Love is a cross. This cross is the universal place where men meet God and begin to understand and accept each other.

The gospels do not use the word *tree* for the cross, but Paul does several times. Peter, too, has it in a sermon reported in Acts 10. We use it in our hymns and poetry as we express what it is we think God is saying to us through the Christ event.

The Biblical story begins with a tree—the tree of the knowledge of good and evil. It deals symbolically with man's first experience of freedom, the freedom to set himself against God, as well as to enjoy God's friendship. W. H. Auden describes how children, a week before Christmas, accidentally stumble upon presents hidden in a closet and instantly grow up as their universe of illusion, fairies and secret happenings dies. The price of having eaten from the tree is also painful but it is constructive pain.

There's also the tree in Psalm 1, where we learn of the man who, because he decides to respond to God and live in the light of God's Commandments, resembles a "tree planted by rivers of water." We, too, must live and grow beside some life-giving stream or our personalities become hard and dry, our ideals chalk and brittle bones on some unmarked Mojave grave of ambition.

In the book of Revelation is written, "In the middle of the street of the city, and on either bank of the river grew the tree of life, bearing twelve fruits, a different kind for each month. The leaves of the tree were for the healing of the nations" (Revelation 22:2 PHILLIPS). The Scriptures both begin and end with the picture of a tree, while at its center there stands the most unusual one of all.

It helps to understand that tree's meaning if we put ourselves, even for a little while, in the place of the crucified and look down upon all things as He did that Friday afternoon.

The world looked then much as it does today. We fly crowds of people through the air, transplant human hearts and publish thousands of books each month but we still are men in distress.

96

Our achievements in transportation and communication, rather than alleviating the problems of war and alienation, have only pointed up how crucial they are. Man still is severed from man by race and economic situation, and also inside so small a unit as the individual family—husband from wife, parent from child. Further, we know we are divided even against ourselves and lack a feeling of inward unity. At least, we seem to have little in the way of calm, and keep wondering who we are. To complicate it more, we are told we are living between the times—between an age which is dying, but not quite dead, and another which is trying to get itself born, but still has only a tiny arm or leg, thus far, thrust out into the world.

The word *reconciliation* is formal and dull-sounding, but no other seems adequate. The name of the game is how to reconcile, how to bring together, in stimulating and beneficial interrelationship, the old and the young, the black and the white, the materially poor and materially rich, the man who wants to protect the past, and the man who is dedicated to change. Sometimes we act as if it were a battle to the death in which one must conquer and absorb the other. That is not the objective. Tension is good. It is the soul of creativity, the condition of growth. War, hate, mistrust, fear and greed are negative forces. These the cross cries out against.

The First Methodist Church of Dallas displayed a ten-foot cross. It was adorned with knives, guns, barbed wire, hypodermic needles and pieces of a smashed car.

It is to our credit that we now appear ready to accept responsibility for building bridges of understanding for mankind. No longer do we blame wars on God, nor try to baptize our hates, nor wallow in a resignation that says man is hopelessly mean. If we care about survival, we had better decide something can be done about it. We cannot do it alone. We cannot do it with mere social engineering. We cannot do it merely by solving the problems of health, housing and education. These are pieces of the puzzle, and we are not entitled to undervalue the secular structures of our common life. Christianity is a gospel, not an instruction manual.

97

It is the Spirit of man, as well as his house, which must be repaired. Christianity begins with an affirmation about what God has done for man. Until that truth is recognized, and responded to, the Christian faith is little more than a beautiful but impracticable ethic. When it is recognized, freedom is born and new life begins.

There's a story of an evangelist exhorting a skid-row audience in the name of a better life. With proper flourish, he summed up his appeal for reform in the words of Kipling's "If," where each thought begins, "If you can." As he finished, a hand went up, and an honest voice inquired: "But what if you can't?"

Most of us can't. We can't, with any consistency, live up to the best we know. In the end, we all wind up on our knees before a stake which seems both to articulate something of our own defeat and to comfort us by saying that if our hearts condemn us, God is greater than our hearts. Sometimes it is hard to get away from the feeling that, rather than molding a brave new world of tomorrow, we are, as a nation and as a society of nations, moving in reverse. It is not the apparent insolubility of war and the prospect of endless urban disorder that act as depressants; it is the deeper loss of confidence in ourselves which comes from confidence in God. Back to God sounds like a trail chant, but it may be our greatest national need.

The cross is God's word of hope to men and nations. It doesn't argue that if things get difficult enough God will bail us out. That's not the hope. Faith is not a last-chance saloon before we cross the border into oblivion. The good news is that God is involved *now*. His power is not power that can be measured in megatons. It cannot be measured at all, only trusted, glimpsed in unusual places and mysterious forms and received with thanksgiving. Dante says it elegantly in one sentence: "His will is our peace."

This tree of endurance is not only a good place to see; it is also an important place to *be* in days like ours. Wrote Georgia Harkness:

I listen to the agony of God
I who am fed, who never went hungry for a day.
I see the dead—the children starved for lack of bread—
I see, and try to pray.

Our world is full of crosses—celluloid and gold, ruby-encrusted, extruded aluminum. It is too filled with religious crosses, but too empty of the crosses upon which man is willing to be hanged in the name of justice and love. "Father forgive them, for they know not what they do." If the Crucified were to look out upon our world today and see us pitted against one another as violently as we are, His Words might very well be the same. Humility may save us. Its source is the suffering servant who became the risen servant. Resurrection, not grief, is our password. The way, though it leads through death, leads to happiness. The tree of sorrow turns into a tree of life. That's both the possibility and the promise of Christ-community and it's welcome information for all the commonwealth of men.

15
A Bulldog May Save Your Life

Who, then, can separate us from the love of Christ? Can trouble do it, or hardship, or persecution, or hunger, or poverty, or danger or death? No, in all these things we have complete victory through him who loved us! For I am certain that nothing can separate us from his love: neither death nor life; neither angels nor other heavenly rulers or powers; neither the present nor the future; neither the world above nor the world below—there is nothing in all creation that will ever be able to separate us from the love of God which is ours through Christ Jesus our Lord (Romans 8:35, 37-39 TEV).

BONNIE BAKER lived the life of a recluse in a large ramshackle house on Ninth Avenue. She had no family, but she did own ten cats. They wandered daily among the dusty furniture, eating from plates scattered everywhere. Even the few people who knew her were a little afraid of Bonnie, and kids in the neighborhood called the place haunted. When, on rare occasions she did venture out, she wore a half-dozen layers of clothing.

One afternoon her house was ignited by a dropped match and a symphony of flames cleared the property. Bonnie, herself, was rescued by the fire department and taken to a nursing home: everyone breathed a sigh of relief.

A legend was retired that day. A problem of the sanitation department was solved. Amid the shouts of the firemen, and the sizzling sound of water hitting the roof, I could not help recalling some of the conversations I had with Bonnie during the previous four years. There had been Calvinists among her forbears, and, as the Presbyterian minister, I always had been welcome at her door.

"Well, it's our minister," she would remark, identifying herself with the straight world.

Early one evening, as I stopped by en route to my own happy supper table, we sat together in the fading daylight watching two kittens scrap over a piece of yellow yarn.

"They're something alive," she had said with a faint smile.

I knew, as I watched the dilapidated furniture being carried out and heard the crowd's laughter that, while in many ways her long isolation had been self-imposed and self-determined, it was the result of those fears of encounter which, at times, infect all men with paranoia. People left Bonnie alone because she gave the impression that that's what she wanted. What she really wanted was love, friendship, understanding, acceptance and inclusion.

The God who stands at the center of the Christian announcement is a God who will not let men alone even if they have said on the surface that they want nothing to do with Him. He refuses to take them at their word. Perhaps it is eyes-on-the-past religion, the church, or the church's plunge into controversy which many now wish to abandon—not God. It also seems clear that millions have come to the conclusion they can live successfully without Him. They simply drop the course. They are not hostile. They do not argue the case of more interesting alternatives. They simply plow ahead with mortgage payments, watch their weight, and meditate upon World War III.

This is understandable, for it is no small thing to become involved with an interfering God who pursues men across the thresholds of their feelings of security and accomplishment. It is normal to avoid this Caller who keeps ringing the doorbell of another self, who stands there, hand against the buzzer even after we've shouted from behind the door that we wish to go on living as we are.

The Bible is filled with stories of men and women who have sought to avoid God. They complained He was unreasonable, or they were too busy—the thing He asked was impossible, or that they were not qualified to obey. Jonah, when he was commanded to preach repentance and hope to the people of Nineveh boarded a ship headed in the opposite direction. Elijah hid in a cave. The cynic in Psalm 14 shrugged and said, "There is no God." Jesus, unsure of his ability to carry out the mission with which he was confronted, went to the desert to think it over.

In the city, privacy is a cherished possession, but we still don't want to be alone. We insulate ourselves, as cleverly as we know how, with the hedges of unlisted telephone numbers and door locks. Solitude is an obvious good, but when we defend ourselves too well against the world we develop our own eccentricities and begin to die. It takes a certain amount of pain to live.

Edward Hale's book *The Man Without a Country* is the story of the young patriot who said in a fit of political disgust, "I wish I might never have to hear of the United States again!" He was punished by having his wish fulfilled.

Who hasn't said something he didn't mean, then realized the value of a relationship because he wasn't taken literally? Proverbs speaks of the friend who sticks closer than a brother. Christians like to apply those words to Jesus. Part of the meaning of His life is that it represents to us the faithfulness of God, God's determination to stay concerned about us and be involved with us, whether we decide He's relevant to our century or not. God cannot be understood in terms of abstract principles, such as perfect purity, truth, or order. He is, rather, the Shepherd searching for the hundredth sheep. He is the Sufferer appealing to men from the cross, even after they have driven a spear through His side. He is the God who will not let us alone even when we have told Him to go away. Paul's letter to the Romans says, ". . . Nothing can separate us from the love of God" (NEB). The exciting thing

101

about these words is that they describe God's decision rather than ours.

How can bondage like that be explained or recommended in the light of what we are told about man's new maturity, about his new ability and obligation to live without God? Thomas Merton helps answer the question.

> The "God" which radical Theology claims to be dead is . . . a God that never lived anyway; a God of hypotheses, a God of pious cliches, a God of formalistic ritual, a God invoked to make comfortable people more pleased with themselves, a God called upon to justify every kind of cruelty and evil and hypocrisy.

Throughout the civilizing process, men have substituted God's will, punishment or vengeance for everything they could not control. Thunder was God pacing the floor in anger, lightning the flashing of His eyes. Floods and famine were divine retribution. Women who died in childbirth were dying as part of His will.

Not all such assigning of responsibility belongs to the distant past. God is still widely thought of as the Star Keeper who runs everything. This does represent partial truth. Jesus reveals the God who loves even the barn sparrow. Adult faith denies God rather than witnesses to Him, when it treats cancer as a providential occurrence rather than a medical problem which men with scientific understanding and concern for each other are called to deal with bravely.

When we are told that God has been preparing us for a time when we must live without Him, we are being warned that we must not attempt to use God as a crutch. This does not add up to a withdrawal of His mercy. It is one thing to say we must discard a warehouse God. A world genuinely come of age only can be fulfilled by accepting responsibility for what happens to it and within it. This does not contradict a bulldog theology based upon the tenacity of persisting love.

Jesus told a story about a man who had unexpected guests one night and was unable to serve a meal because his cupboard was empty. He went to his neighbor's, hoping to borrow enough bread for a simple meal. The house was dark: it was late. He knocked but there was no answer. He knocked a second and then a third time. Silence. As he waited there in the chill and darkness, tides of humiliation and embarrassment began to rise within him. In a final desperate effort he doubled his fist and pounded savagely upon the door; with his other hand he rattled the lock. Finally he heard a low voice from within, "What do you want?"

The man explained his emergency.

"Go away," said the neighbor sleepily, annoyed. "It's past midnight. We're all in bed."

With this encouragement the host pressed his case and the neighbor was at last persuaded to open the door and furnish the needed supplies.

Why God continues to try is an unfathomable mystery. Badger Clark asks

> Why don't you quit
> Crumple it all and dream again! But no;
> Bondage, brutality, and war, and woe,
> The sot, the fool, the tyrant and the mob—
> Dear God, how you must love your job!

Our giving up is somewhat easier to understand. Out of our fatigue, we enter periods when belief dies, when faith turns in its resignation (with carbon copies) to the whole enterprise. To admit less is to be dishonest, but morning returns and we begin again each day to be Christian.

The German martyr, Dietrich Bonhoeffer, had what he might have called a working faith in God at the time he was arrested and imprisoned by the Gestapo. He expected settlement of his case within six weeks at the most. After two years in jail his death was becoming the predictably certain outcome of charges against him. His conclusions, as to how God may be involved in history and in what forms His power is present, changed. As the guards led him out of his cell to be hanged that morning in April of 1945, his trust was in the same God, but now his faith had a new maturity and toughness.

We don't want to be left alone. There are times when we think

103

we would like to be freed from the demands, and from the gaze that seems to ask, "Well?" Such wishes are as mistaken and illusory as Bonnie Baker's preference for solitude. Meantime, God says, "Let Me in. Break out some refreshment; set the table for two; light a candle." The worst thing that could ever happen to you, the worst news that could ever come to you, would be the message that God had taken you at your word and decided to leave you alone.

16

Awe Is Our Final Protection

O world, I cannot hold thee close enough!
Thy winds, thy wide gray skies!
Thy mists, that roll and rise!
Thy woods, this autumn day, that ache and sag
And all but cry with color. That gaunt crag
To crush! To lift the lean of that black bluff!
World, world, I cannot get thee close enough!

EDNA ST. VINCENT MILLAY

WE HAVE BEEN trying to put our arms around the city. In Edna Millay's poem she tries to put her arms around the world, and squeeze it hard against her as we are inclined to do with persons we love. In Christmas we feel that way about a certain truth—a truth staged in the symbols of star and stable, shepherds, a troubled husband, a mystified young mother-in-waiting, a busy innkeeper, astrologers from the East, and a Baby Boy who becomes true man. Each December we hold this truth up again to prominent view as our hearts exclaim

O God, I cannot praise You near enough
Your love, Your message in a star

104

Your tired couple, manger cry, and wise men from afar.
Your overture! The earth tonight is chorus bathed,
A million arrows slit the sky,
And men at last stop shouting why,
Sun! Son! I see God's orange rim!

Father Louis (Thomas Merton) said of the first mass he celebrated as a priest, "My heart was stunned."

Awe is our final protection. In a time when we seem to be
experiencing disenchantment with ourselves, as man accepts more
and more of the world as his responsibility and the arc of God's
responsibility seems to grow rapidly less, we can be saved from
despair and the feeling that we are living in a deserted universe
by awe. An age without awe is an age of unrelieved anxiety.

The Christmas story was written from this side of Calvary. Its
awe is produced, not just by a beautiful Child born in a barn, but
also by an adult Jesus who declared, "He who has seen me has seen
the Father." The faith that delivers us out of a blasé, ho-hum, so-
what-else-is-new frame of mind has its grounding, not just in the
story of this birth, but in the fullness of an event which says God is!
God cares! So long as God is, we cannot settle for a squirrel-cage
definition of life.

Those who describe the increasing secularization of life are not
enemies of awe; instead, they invite men to experience awe in
fresh ways. They tell us things we don't like to hear. People who
love us often do that. In our times, we face as much revolutionary
change in theology as in technology. Conversations about secularity
are not a conspiracy to take away from us a sense of awe.

For early man, life itself was mystery—birth and death, nation-
hood, trees, streaks of lightning, rainbows, illnesses, wars, famine,
the starlit spaces. God was the cause of everything. The universe
was spirit filled. The sky was alive with angels and demons. Then
came modern science, and with it the proprietorship of man. He
stopped attributing floods to divine wrath and began building
dams; he stopped interpreting polio as punishment and began
eradicating it with vaccines. This process, multiplied over and
over again, has forced religion into a revised understanding of
what God and man have to do with each other. There is nothing

105

demonic about this process and nothing about it which needs to be fatal to awe, nor feared as the adversary of faith. Still, awe will be of a different kind.

In Bethlehem there is a basis for an awe which remains intact, which remains inwardly healing and outwardly true.

Christmas is two things.

First, it is the story of God's love for man, declaring that God loved the world and moved within history's processes to rescue it.

Second, it is a communication about how God's coming occurs—about His style, and how He meets men in common stuff and lowly circumstances. These are truths the scientific revolution has not changed, has no desire to change, has no power to change.

Christmas says God is Love, and that Love meets us in the beauty and the magnetism of man's own helplessness as a baby in the night, as a man bleeding on a cross.

This God is not dead.

Sinclair Lewis once dared God, in the midst of a public address, to strike him dead. When nothing happened he said in effect, "There! You see: there is no such God."

Gracie Hegger Lewis criticizes the Associated Press interpretation of Sinclair Lewis' dramatic action saying that Lewis was intent to show that God is not the avenging god of this man's imagination.

Dr. George Buttrick, reacting to the story in *Sermons Preached in a University Church* says

> But, of course, the argument could have gone in the other direction, as indeed Sinclair Lewis was there intent to prove: "Only a God of infinite patience and love would endure that nonsense and let him go on living." As for proofs, there is one kind of proof for potatoes, another for poems, another for persons, and another for God. Beyond all proofs and in lack of them we must go on living. What we need is a strategy rather than a proof, a strategy and a certain valor of the spirit.

It is a life both of awe and action that the bells of Christmas call. We are left without peace until we go, as our fathers did before us, to kneel beside them in the straw.

106

17

The Secular City Says Its Prayers

I'm tired, God. The space suit is heavy and the voyage has been long. Thanks for letting us get here safely. Some said getting here would be a waste of time and money, a diversion of the nation's energies from more important goals. I wish they could be here tonight with us. The silence is as beautiful as life. I am not afraid.

They were right about the moon being mostly a cold rock, following the earth around like a little brother. It's not like a field of daisies, or the face of my son, but it's the greatest moment I've ever known—maybe the greatest in the history of man, like creation beginning all over!

I don't know whether I can sleep. I'm trembling. I'm anxious to do everything expected of me. There are many experiments and we need rest to do them well. Watch over us a little while.

Let our first words here be words of peace.

A BEDTIME PRAYER FOR THE FIRST NIGHT ON THE MOON.

MODERN MAN does not appear to be interested in prayer, but he is interested in God. Whatever else is in, prayer is out, unless it gets renamed.

Prayer often has been looked upon as the tool of the fainthearted, a substitute for action, primitive dependency.

A brokenhearted father looked down into a casket at the lifeless body of his child, a nine-year-old daughter who, the day before, had skipped rope on the patio while he repaired a broken window sash.

"Do you want me to pray?" I asked, from just behind where the aggrieved father stood.

"I would rather that you cursed!"

Books on the inner life often begin with reference to the fact that man is incurably religious, and that all men pray, sometime. That's getting to be a tough statement to defend. All men wonder, all men engage in a quest for an explanation of themselves and the universe, but the knowledge explosion has left prayer far back. Along with the institutional church, prayer seems to be moving steadily toward the outer edges of human enterprise. This is happening at the very moment when persons are pleading for perspective in which to set their amazing new technology.

There was a time when the preacher's prayers on Sunday morning were among the week's liveliest events. In "Drums Along The Mohawk" the Reverend Mr. Rozencrantz prays:

O Almighty God, we are thinking right now of Mary Marte Wollaber. She is just fifteen years old, but she is going with one of the soldiers at Fort Dayton. He is a Massachusetts man, O God, and it has come to my attention that he is married in the town of Hingham. I have had her father and mother talk to her, I have talked to her myself, but she won't pay any attention. We ask Thy help, God Almighty, in bringing her back to the path of virtue, from which we believe she has strayed pretty far.

O Almighty God, you have brought us an early spring; keep off the frost until the fruit is set. O Lord, the English Codlin Nicholas Herkimer has grafted onto his Indian apple tree has bloomed this year. May it bear fruit. It is a wonderful example of Thy ways, and worth our going to see, and Nicholas Herkimer will show it to anybody.

O Almighty God, we ask Thy compassion for all of us who are in sickness. We ask it for Peter Paris who got the flux real bad. His Uncle Isaac Paris sent the news up to us and asks our prayers and says that he has got a new supply of calicos, French reds, Russias, fancy han'chers, some new hats and heavy boots, scythes and grindstones . . .

108

O God Almighty, our own Colonel Peter Bellinger wants the fourth company to muster at Dayton tomorrow, June sixteenth. . . ."

We would need to except from our list prayers by such rare spirits as Malcom Boyd, Michel Quoist and Carl Burke, but for the most part, the idea of prayer invokes little feeling of awe.

Public prayers are often trite, and tied, both in spirit and in language, and addressed to an age that has disappeared. Most of us pray infrequently, unsatisfyingly and on many days not at all. In the same breath, we acknowledge something else; our desire for God was never greater.

University courses in religion have record enrollments. Youths reject material success and convenience as representing the most important values of their lives, but have a keen interest in meditation. Cities beg for alternatives to violence, and for political solutions grounded in forgiveness, love and trust. Poets summon men to new vocations of gentleness. Attempts are being made on a wide front to breathe health back into the American dream.

Space-age man may not be incurably religious, but he is incurably spiritual—a difference these times have exposed. He may have decided he can live adequately without worship, without dogmas, without an assurance of life beyond, but, as spirit, he is bound to God forever.

I believe He is capable of falling back in love with prayer, but only if the word describes the full opening of his life to the fullness of the world and its possibilities.

This will not happen if prayer is understood to be an escape. Wrote Jeremiah

Thus says the Lord of hosts, the God of Israel, Amend your ways and your doings, and I will let you dwell in this place. Do not trust in these deceptive words: "This is the temple of the Lord, the temple of the Lord, the temple of the Lord." For if you truly amend your ways and your doings, if you truly execute justice one with another . . . then I will let you dwell . . . in the land that I gave of old to your fathers. . . . (Jeremiah: 7:3-5 RSV).

This means, do not go around saying, "Let us pray, let us pray," if, in the same moment, you shut your eyes and close your ears to the pain, the tragedy and the lostness of persons around you.

That's what put prayer out of style. The Now generation has faced the fact that men can go on praying in the same old places with the same old words, generation after generation, without making any real difference. While praying went on, racial injustices went unchallenged. There were few people praying to help Nat Turner's revolution succeed. Men prayed on Sunday, and abused each other on Monday. That was hard on prayer's reputation.

This is also a time when men's thoughts about God are unclear. That's another discouragement. We reject the Man upstairs. We do not know where to go. We hunger for a beyondness to life, but don't know how to visualize it. We do not know how to pray.

Still, Christians speak in the name of Jesus to a Hearer whose existence they cannot confirm. On bent knees and with lowered heads, they ponder Him, remembering His firmness and sympathy, His humor, death, patience and resurrection. They know that, through such images, their faith touches part of the divine garments and they are healed.

Studdert-Kennedy had this process in mind when he wrote

The splendid spirit can run through the men who really pray, like a stream of living fire, out into the world of men and women who need just that, and only that, for with that comes all that's best worth having in this world.

Jesus prayed often. Our imagination is kindled by the New Testament's references to his rising early in the morning, while it was still dark, and going off alone for private encounter. Howard Thurman, contemporary mystic, adds another side:

The most precious time for the Master was at the close of day. This was the time for the long breath, when all the fragments left by the commonplace, all the little hurts and big aches came to demand, and voices that had been stilled by the long day's work could be the deep sharing of innermost secrets and laying bare of heart and mind. . . .

110

What, though, must characterize the prayers of man in the secular city, if they are to be meaningful, satisfying?

We really cannot pray if our minds are made up in advance. Prayer is openness. Prayer can return to the life of our society only when it once again becomes equated with the new possibilities that a new age of history contains.

If we are to pray again, we also must have those qualities of the spirit that precede prayer. If we honestly care about others, if we are grateful to God for His gifts, prayer won't be something imposed from the outside.

Prayer must enfold the world. There is no turning back on this direction in man's understanding of faith. God's world is here to be loved, nurtured, shaped. Prayer, which amounts to copping out on human responsibility, warrants no resurrection.

Prayer is part of commitment. Its content is dependent upon the substance of commitment, and this is concerned strongly with justice and understanding between men. It is not a substitute for the servant life, any more than unselfish deeds are a substitute for a life within.

Jesus remains our most valuable source of our insight about those things for which we ought to pray, and things for which we ought not to pray. He is the Lord of choice.

Prayer is communication. As encounter with God, it makes us more competent to encounter one another, and thus achieve community.

One of the most valid comments on prayer I know is by a man who packed several lifetimes into his thirty-four years. From a hospital bed in Hong Kong, Dr. Thomas Dooley, on December 2, 1960, wrote a letter to one of his favorite teachers at Notre Dame. On a portable typewriter supported by his knees, he pounded out some last sentences to a man he was sure would understand.

It has become pretty definite that the cancer has spread to the lumbar vertebrae, accounting for all the back problems over the last two months. I have monstrous phantoms . . . as all men do. But I try to exorcise them with all the fury of the Middle Ages. And inside and outside the wind blows. . . .

111

But when the time comes, like now, then the storm around me does not matter. The winds within me do not matter. Nothing human or earthy can touch me.

A wilder storm of peace gathers in my heart. What seems unpossessable I can possess. What seems unfathomable I fathom. What is unutterable, I can utter. Because I can pray. I can communicate. How do people endure anything on earth if they cannot have God?

Death came a few weeks later. Today more than a hundred medical men are carrying on the healing ministry he began. Maybe the problems of America's cities will yield also to prayer's glorious leverage.

18
Look Out for Confidence Men

Why set this hunger for eternity
To gnaw my heart-strings through,
                    if death ends all?
If death be death, then evil must be good,
Wrong must be right and beauty ugliness.
God is a Judas who betrays His friend,
And with a kiss damns all the world to hell,
If Christ came not again. . . .
But I go laughing in my heart. . . .

G. A. STUDDERT-KENNEDY

CONFIDENCE MEN always have been a part of city life. They are poised guys who are faced, so they say, with the possibility of becoming wealthy overnight. All that stands between them and instant fortune, which they are willing to share, is a modest amount of assistance—yours! For unsuspecting thousands, a helping hand has become a severed arm.

There are other kinds of con men in the city, too, men who deal, not in frauds, but in faith. This faith is celebrated by millions every day, but its most eloquent expression occurs on Easter Day.

Easter recalls an event, the historic details of which are lost forever in the mists of mystery. All there is to measure it by are its effects. Those effects have been so enormous and pervasive no man with booked passage on this ship of fools can ignore it.

It mixes thoughts of death and life. It brings back both soothing and ache-producing memories of persons we have loved, and reminds us how fragile the whole thing is, as if life were made out of pie crust that falls apart at our touch. The Kirkeby is a handsome high-rise office building across the street. Mr. Kirkeby died in a plane crash a few weeks before it was finished. The building is a parable of all existence. We are strangers on the earth. To take a single day for granted is to exaggerate our grip.

The Resurrection presents many problems and we cannot solve them. They do not fit a positivistic age. They defy universal laws. At the same time they form the basis of the Easter life—life based on the conviction that God is love, and that that love encompasses death. Easter is hard news. It is a place to stand, a creed by which to live. It is freedom to enjoy. It is a breeze blowing through the stale houses of our pride, selfishness, envy, fear and resentment. It begins back in the shadows of an incredible happening, but it doesn't stay there. It is part of the miracle of the present, an energy that brings the church together in a spirit of rejoicing, which, if we will give it a chance, will reunite the whole splintered family of man. Easter is not a guessing game. It is a confidence game, confidence in God as Lord of history.

The victory is as close as our fingertips, for Easter is not based upon museum evidence. It is not something written on a scrap of paper. It is contemporary people. It is the Easter life being lived before our eyes.

Often it is a quiet thing, expressing itself without words. When men learn to put their confidence in God, in spite of a world in which God often seems to be missing, they become confident in new ways.

It is the conviction that God is at work in the world, and we are not sure of the ways. It appears to have something to do with suffering. Easter torn apart from Good Friday is a ghost town, little more than an annual wistfulness. It is a confidence that takes away from us the excuse that we didn't know any better. It makes us want to dress up in pastels, but it also makes us hurt. All living of any consequence is based upon a certain amount of pain.

A second word that helps profile the Easter life is freedom. Because of its confidence it is also the free life.

We are staggered by death. It isn't that we are afraid of the last fifteen minutes. It's rather fear that neither death nor life has any abiding significance. We search for meaning in our jobs, in sexual encounters, in the arts. Another drink may help us forget for awhile, but one security after another eventually is abandoned. Like the Son of God, we all come, in our time, to a desert of loneliness not knowing we have stumbled onto the doorstep of freedom, almost, as if it were, by accident. Freedom begins at a point where other things die.

Dr. King, the night before his death, told the world he had seen the Promised Land. His writings made clear that he knew it was not a land put together out of automobile chrome, television sets and stomach stuffings. The promised land is a land in which each man walks tall because he is a man, where he is not afraid of himself nor his neighbors, where he is not ignorant, nor caught in technological helplessness, where he is bound to the image of God upon his brow rather than to the twisted images of a racist past to which all have contributed something. The only race that really matters is the human race.

The Easter life is the free life because it invites men to rest in God's will, not in their own cleverness and bravery. Everything that suffers from rigidity, tenseness, or inability to adapt to change is now termed uptight. The risen life is the opposite of that. It has a gaiety which laughs at change. It understands the piecrust character of life and doesn't try to turn it into steel, nor does it compromise its divine liberty by pulling heavy baggage behind it as it goes.

It is in the face of death that a man begins to make decisions about the things that are really important. Eddie Rickenbacker tells a story about his crippled B-17 during World War II. When he and his crew realized they were going to crash, they began to empty the cabin of all the things they knew would lighten the ship. Finally, Rickenbacker made a decision to throw out his briefcase full of secret papers. The tragedy is that most of us spend more time preparing for a two-week vacation than we do for eternity. Learning to die is learning to live. Coming to terms with death, locating it inside not outside of the wisdom of God, is to enter the house of Easter.

A resurrection quality of being also involves discovery. One of Luke's best sentences is in telling how on that first Sunday night, Jesus revealed himself to the eleven in the breaking of bread. As the Holy Communion reminds us, the place to look for Him is in common things. This is confidence, freedom and discovery rolled into one—into the single reality that God is alive. If we would discover Him and have Him discover us, it will be in the raw materials of daily decision, in the rebuilding of our cities and our society, in making our neighborhoods not all white but all American, in finding good in each other's faces, in ecstasy and pain, in the tympanies of the surf, in the noise of the freeway, in all the little nobilities and encounters which shout life is more than meat, and the body more than clothing.

There is a pseudo-Christianity that is afraid of life. It distrusts everything that is different. It is stiff and not free. It is so busy playing religion, it never gets the message about the resurrection of the body. James Baldwin has a word for this distortion. "To be sensual, I think is to respect and rejoice in the force of life, of life itself, and to be *present* in all that one does, from the effort of loving to the breaking of bread. . . . Something very sinister happens to the people of a country when they begin to distrust their own re-actions as deeply as they do here, and become joyless as they have become."

The world has not been able to recognize a surplus of joy in the institutional church. It has noticed more joy in the pub than in the pew. Daily at Synanon's Santa Monica drug rehabilitation center there is a hoop-la. It's a hybrid between a dance and group calisthenics. During the hoop-la, each participant moves rhythmically to a kind of exhilarating music, expressing his own inner condition and

115

desire for rapport with life. It is obvious to a spectator that each is discovering something liberating he hadn't known before. Addiction is a tough slavery. Now there appears some faintly-marked path back into the light.

This is the discovery all men can make. They do not discover it by joining the church, nor by answering someone else's question about belief in Jesus Christ. The evidence points the other way. The church hasn't proved on any large scale that it knows what the new life is all about. It is more often afraid, suspicious, tradition-oriented—too busy to communicate, too turned in upon itself to unbend and love.

There are all kinds of confidence games from finding sunken treasure to producing the missing heir. Easter recognizes a different way of being conned. Perhaps it's silly to call it that, but players have to suit up for it and play with all their hearts. To boycott it is to die. To claim it is to live and cross the river singing.

IV
DON'T HIT PEDESTRIANS
IN THE CROSSWALK

19

I Don't Want to Live in the Zoo, but the Jungle Sounds Pretty Good

The great Hindu saint of the nineteenth century, Radikrishna told a fable about a motherless tiger cub who was adopted by goats and brought up by them to speak their language, emulate their ways, eat their food, and in general to believe he was a goat himself. Then one day a king tiger came along, and when all the goats scattered in fear, the young tiger was left alone to confront him, afraid and yet somehow not afraid. The king tiger asked him what he meant by his unseemly masquerade, but all the young one could do in response was to bleat nervously and continue nibbling at the grass. So the tiger carried him to a pool where he forced him to look at their two reflections side by side and draw his own conclusions. When this failed, he offered him his first piece of raw meat. At first the young tiger recoiled from the unfamiliar taste of it, but then as he ate more and began to feel it warming his blood, the truth gradually became clear to him. Lashing his tail and digging his claws into the ground, the young beast finally raised his head high, and the jungle trembled at the sound of his exultant roar.

FREDERICK BUECHNER

A MAN WHO looks at Jesus has brought home to him a special kind of knowledge about himself. He realizes God has created him for possibilities he may have forgotten. He has become so used to acting like a goat, the fact that he was born a tiger has all but vanished from his consciousness. Tigers have a way of shouting to us, Be like me! Be strong! Walk in strange jungles! Be colorful! Be unafraid of your enemies! Roar with confidence! Get out of that domesticated, dull situation. Break out of that mold of timidity! Begin stalking

119

life! Begin acting as if there were a place in this universe which belongs to you! Be a tiger, not a pussycat!

Cheetah is a younger generation nightclub. Cougar is a hot sports car that has young buyers drooling. Tigers seem to sell everything from gasoline to cologne, from blazers to motorboats.

Long before Madison Avenue discovered the appeal of the tiger as a virile advertising symbol, T.S. Eliot wrote that in the juvenescence of the year comes Christ the Tiger. Is this not what the gospel also suggests—that what we are seeking, whether we know it or not, is an adventuresome life under God, a life modeled after the Carpenter? Why have we pictured Jesus so often as a pussycat? What young man honestly hungers to be *like* the Nazarene? None, because the authentic Jesus with steel in his eyes and passion in his steps is smothered by a carload of lesser images the church has tolerated to its shame.

In some ways it is easier to look at Jesus and say, "I see what God is like" than to say "I see who man is." The hard thrust of the United Presbyterian Confession of 1967 is apparent with the first sentence. "In Jesus of Nazareth true humanity was realized once for all." This is not all it says about the mystery of His person. It says more. It presents Him as the Word made Flesh, but first it exalts Him as Man.

What God is trying to communicate in Jesus might add up to this, "Look at my Son. See His courage. See His concern for the poor and the disheartened. Look at His ability to see, even in pain, important reasons to exist. See His love of hills and sea and children. Notice His freedom from all that is artificial and false. Touch the hands that healed the sick. Sense His full embrace of life as gift. Stand beside Him. Gaze with Him into the pool of God and learn anew the basis of your liberty and the reason for your birth."

Having understood Him as a man, our minds are ready to move into bluer water. The Old Testament prepares us by telling us about a God who, not only created a world of men, but continues to be concerned with them in a loving and responsible way. God first gave men laws, principles of integrity, canons of relationship, rules for determining the ingredients of a meaningful life, then He added the counsel of the prophets. This was God still evidencing His involvement, His self-investment. Then, when all appeared to be mired down in failure, Jesus came and history turned a corner. His impact was so great and continues so radical, that labels or theologies cannot encompass its full meaning. In Him, faith sees not just additional evidence of God's participation in human life; it sees Jesus as the crucial disclosure, a movement within history with power to rescue man forever from nonidentity, and death. The cry which comes sounding through the centuries, and which seems to be greater than any one age, is that in Jesus, God has entered with such authority and grace that the only way we can describe what has occurred is by saying that, in Jesus, God has come to men. This is no peddler of a new religion. Religions are systems or formulas, but the One who is followed by the Christian church judges all religions, Christianity included. God cannot be harbored in any system or institution. He is a tiger, not a tethered goat.

The Bible does not teach the Trinity (Father, Son and Holy Spirit) as explicit doctrine, but it introduces us to a God who meets us on three different levels of experience. We encounter the order of the universe and use the human term *Father* to explain God as Source and Sustainer. Another confrontation occurs on the level of history through an historical Man who split time in half. This is God, too—God communicating Himself vividly. He is not two Gods, rather one Lord, whose Being and Love are transmitted in different languages. Even two dimensions do not contain the full frequency of this Voice. God meets us, not only in the origin of life as a Father, and not uniquely in the dynamics of history, as a Son, but He also touches our understanding, and ministers to our needs in an ultrapersonal and immediate activity we name Spirit. Holy Spirit means God with us now, as an omnipresent personalized presence, a presence we sometimes know as comfort, sometimes as discomfort.

Three young men, each barely twenty, reported to a meeting of the Synod of California. Each was sensitive and intelligent. Each had been through his own Gethsemane over the war in Viet Nam. One had been wounded in battle three times. Another had returned his draft card and indicated a readiness to take the consequences. His knowledge of Asian political history was impressive. The third was equally knowledgeable and sensitive to the emotion of

121

duty, having been in Hiroshima as a university exchange student on the twentieth anniversary of the dropping of the bomb. He told how he had since changed his view and petitioned the government for the return of his draft card in order to fulfill whatever military responsibility he may be assigned.

Here is the complete spectrum of moral judgment, and the church does not call one right, the other wrong. In each testimony is the ingredient of passion, the proof of caring, and that's as much as the church can say. There is no way of gauging ultimate correctness. That's why the doctrine of the Spirit is the most important teaching of all.

The option not open is indifference. Indifference is the enemy of passion and the highway to death. Jesus would rather be hated than ignored and so would we. Hate at least carries some kind of meaning in reverse. Faith, hope and love are the positive possibilities, and nothing can down them. In *The First Born* Moses addresses Pharaoh:

> So they bring about
> The enormity of Egypt. Is that the full
> Ambition of your gods? Egypt is only
> One golden eruption of time, one flying spark
> Attempting the ultimate fire. But who can say
> What secrets my race has, what unworked seams
> Of consciousness in mind and soul? Deny
> Life to itself and life will harness and ride you
> To its purpose. My people shall become themselves,
> By reason of their god who speaks within them.
> What I ask is that I may lead them peaceably
> Into the wilderness for a space, to find
> Their God and so become living men at last.

CHRISTOPHER FRY

Thirteen hundred years elapse and another Man, with two timbers on His back, is making His way toward the public dump where He is to be executed for subversion. If the cross does nothing else for us, it leaves us with His question, "What in my life has such preemptive importance? Anything at all?" We will fight to

122

defend our homes, our land against invading aggressors. Is that all? Are our extremities of concern backed up that far against instinct?

Today many people find the church incredibly dull. Perhaps the reason is because it presents so little choice between itself and anything else. Everything is colored gray. This could attest to honesty, too, for life as a whole is no simpler than Viet Nam. Faith argues that we do not need to wait for life to clear up before we choose God and offer Him a place in our systems of responsibility and value.

History will come and go. The clock will spin round and round. The earth will grow older and colder. We will stumble, fall, rise, walk, stumble again, but through all we can commit ourselves to allowing God's purposes to become the passion, the joy, and confidence of the journey.

Nineteen-year-old RCAF pilot, John Magee, had parents who were missionaries in China. One Sunday night, in a country church I read his verse "High Flight" as part of a sermon. Afterwards a little bent woman shuffled forward and said, "I knew John as a boy. We lived next door to the Magees in Nanking for four years." Composed while flying thirty thousand feet over the earth, it has tiger stripes of feeling all through it.

Oh! I have slipped the surly bonds of earth,
And danced the skies on laughter-silvered wings;
Sunward I've climbed and joined the tumbling mirth
Of sun-split clouds—and done a hundred things
You have not dreamed of—wheeled and soared and swung
High in the sunlit silence. Hov'ring there,
I've chased the shouting wind along and flung
My eager craft through footless halls of air.

Up, up the long delirious, burning blue
I've topped the wind-swept heights with easy grace,
Where never lark, or even eagle, flew;
And, while with silent, lifting mind I've trod
The high untrespassed sanctity of space,
Put out my hand, and touched the face of God.

123

There's much to be passionate about, to be eager about, to throw your life away for, to work for, to suffer for, to die for.

"Christians," writes Robert Nelson, "are called to be optimists without illusions, pessimists without despair." He remarks on the tremendous gulf which divides the life of men today. The haves, most of whom, he says, live north of a latitudinal line that is close to Nagasaki, Cairo and Fort Worth, are the human minority. The have-not majority lives south of this line, and the rich get richer and the poor get poorer with each succeeding year. Arguments against a public handout do not cancel out some other words. "I assure you that whatever you did for the humblest of my brothers you did for me" (Matthew 25:40 PHILLIPS).

This is also a time for looking in another direction—within. Therein lies tinder, too, a place to blow upon our souls and bring forth bright colors of renewal. Before we can love others, we must first love ourselves. We learn to love ourselves by taking ourselves seriously, by coming to believe that our lives matter, by recognizing that, through our passion, God's mercy, God's love, God's help is released.

There is a gravestone in Carlisle, Kentucky, on which in letters two inches high this strange inscription appears, "His life was a failure, he died without money." Tourists hearing of the curiosity leave the main highway and detour for several miles to take pictures. When the laughing is over, we still have to put together our rebuttal. "My life, hopefully, is a success because . . . because . . . because. . . ." Here we get hung up.

If Jesus is a Tiger who reminds us that we were born for greatness, even though we have settled on lesser vocations, then God, too, is a Ringmaster whose business is training men for useful living, and inviting them to take part, with Him, in the Greatest Show on Earth.

20
Not All Battles Are Worth Winning

. . . the way should be easy but it is not. I have, first of all, the problem of disengaging myself from certain emotional stances that I now see to be, quite literally, childish in origin. This is something that I have to work out for myself, but happily I am beginning to see the lights of a town in the distance.

The other problem—wouldn't you know it?—is intellectual. The closest I can come to Christianity at present is a Unitarianism that does not seem to me truly Christian at all. But I have the feeling that seeing the lights of the town at the end of the first road is far more important.

I am really looking but just need more time. Those lights, those lights!

A personal letter in response to a church invitation.

AT A SERVICE CLUB LUNCHEON one day theologian George Buttrick was present as a guest-speaker. A man near him at the table, realizing Dr. Buttrick's eminence as a writer and former preacher at Harvard Chapel, sought to engage him in conversation.

"As for me, I don't go to church much," he said, "I guess my religion is just the Sermon on the Mount."

"I didn't know anyone had been able to live up to *that* religion even for five minutes," said Buttrick with friendly irony.

Three phrases of the master commentary on personal ethics help to state the problem.

. . . if any one strikes you on the right cheek, turn to him the other also;

125

and if any one would sue you and take your coat, let him have your cloak as well;

and if any one forces you to go one mile, go with him two miles (Matthew 5:39-41 RSV).

What they have in common is the willingness to lose a battle in order to win a war. The war, or conflict, is the struggle to be a son of God and a maximum human being.

It is an old chestnut, "I won the battle but lost the war," but it contains part of the gospel and some of the cross. It's no fun getting slapped. It seems to make no sense at all to give in to an adversary at law, and not only to lose the argument and therefore your shirt, but to turn around and give up your jacket, too, and your shoes and your underwear. If a Roman official should press you into service, making you walk a mile on business which is not your own, and you should offer to go twice that distance—well, how big a fool can a man be?

This is what makes the Christian faith interesting. It always gives more than it is asked to give. It goes beyond the limits of what is required legally. It does all sorts of surprising things, such as inviting men to love their enemies and to overcome evil with good.

Sometimes it inspires men to give in (even when they remain convinced that they are right), because they see some larger good involved, which is greater than their pride or their vindication.

This kind of flexibility can be, and often is, a sign of strength rather than of weakness. It can be an expression of freedom, freedom from the necessity of always having to be right.

A New Yorker article about newscaster Chet Huntley presented him as a very superior person. The profile noted that when Huntley feels he is right about something, he is exceedingly stubborn and unwilling to give ground. In the late 1950's, during the Hungarian crisis when many cities of eastern Europe were in the news daily, Huntley had several occasions on which he was required to mention the city of Budapest. He called it, quite accurately, Budapesht. This bothered some of the top NBC management, and he was asked to use the more common pronunciation, Budapest, but the

126

famous newsman would not give in. He was certain that he was right.

Such stubbornness is in the Christian tradition. It evidences character. It can mean exemplary courage. I do not argue that, but that's not the whole story of Christian behavior. We can wind up winning the battle, and still lose the war. We may vindicate ourselves, prove a point, conquer our opponent, but we also may sacrifice some other great good in the process of gaining the victory.

The best known example is the salesman who gets into an argument with a customer over the merit of the product he is selling and conquers with his logic, but at the price of the sale. Sometimes integrity demands that. Jesus didn't go around always trying to please people, or to keep from offending them in order to make sales. He did say that if a man strikes you on the right cheek, turn to him your left; if a man takes away your coat, give him your cloak also; if he demands you walk a mile for him, walk two miles. This adds up to something extra. It says something about small defeats or concessions in the interest of larger triumphs.

When my father was fifty-six years old, he already had spent forty years of his life on the Rock Island Railroad. He had dropped out of school as a young man and taken a job as a section hand. He loved the railroading life. It was a romantic business for him with the trains whistling through the night, carrying the grain, the automobiles, the petroleum of the nation back and forth across the breast of America. He also loved the creosote ties, the heavy steel, the snowplows in the winter, the emergency calls at 3 A.M., the dignity of hard work and a chance to observe nature at first hand. He loved his calling and he was good at it. He was honest and tough and always fair with his men.

One day a man who was over him in authority did something that he, my father, thought was unfair. It involved a technical rule which, according to this supervisor, my father had broken. It had nothing to do with the safety of the trains, but it was a rule, nevertheless. Mr. Ray was new to his position and he was determined to operate a tight ship. If any rules were broken, he would see that discipline was meted out.

As for the violation of which he accused my father, and of which my father was probably guilty, he was determined to teach him a

127

lesson. He advised by letter that he was taking my father out of service for thirty days. It was not a severe punishment, but it was severe to my father's pride and sense of responsibility. He was deeply committed to his work and to the best interests of his employer. He was no minimum producer, constantly worried about whether or not he was doing something beyond that for which he was being paid. He was the opposite, and when he was told that he was to be punished by a man who barely knew him, he objected.

A disciplinary hearing was scheduled at which time my dad was to be given the chance to defend himself. He was so wounded by these circumstances, and what seemed to him the unjustness of the action taken, that he resigned. He turned in his pass; he left the railroad forever.

I, of course, was much younger then, and I took my father's side. I defended his rightness with intense passion. When he resigned, rather than submit to what I also believed was a bad show, I praised his judgment. No one was going to push Pop around, no sir!

We won the prime battle, but as I reflect upon the years that followed—the anguish, the longing for his work and his friends, the disorientation at age fifty-six—it seemed he was too old for new beginnings and I believe we lost the war. I think I helped him lose it. I believe if I were doing it over, I would be inclined to say, "Dad, you're right. I know you're right. It isn't fair! All of us who know you and love you know of your keen devotion and sense of duty, and that's all that matters. What the people who do not know you may think, or what judgments they arrive at, is not important. Let's take the punishment, deserved or undeserved, and then forget it. These thirty days will soon be over; they are as nothing compared to a lifetime. Let's lose this battle and be philosophical about it. It's more important to win the war."

If this is personal, the dilemma is not. It is as common as a sunny day in California, for we are all involved in arguments, disagreements, etc., which we do not like to lose. Sometimes this is with an employer, more often it is with a friend, or a wife, or a husband, or a neighbor. Things get snarled up. It takes extraordinary stuff to go ahead and die a little in the name of setting things right, just as it sometimes takes unusual courage to change your mind or to admit a mistake. Even that sort of courage is rare, but an even more advanced order of courage is to go ahead and take your defeat, even when something in your heart tells you that you don't have it coming.

A minister has his own problems. He also becomes involved and acquainted with the problems of others. Many times this involves a standoff between two people or parties, neither of whom is willing to raise the flag of surrender. When that becomes your problem, your dilemma, try to remember that to run up the flag isn't always a sign of weakness. There are times when it's a sign of greatness—that is, if the Sermon on the Mount is to be believed, and I believe it is. If you have to face up to something terribly embarrassing, be comforted, the public mind quickly moves on to new scandals.

Dr. Louis Evans, former minister of the First Presbyterian Church in Hollywood, says that the six most important words in a marriage are, "I was wrong. I am sorry." These words, says Evans, can work all kinds of miracles between people.

The cross embodies both truths. There is the refusal to compromise, to break, to sell out. At the same time there is a massive readiness to forgive, to overlook, to experience loss on behalf of gain.

What the New Testament cries out against is the sin of average living in a hard-fisted legalism which says that these are my rights, this is all you can expect, this is all you're going to get. The call of Jesus Christ is the call to a life of good measure, pressed down, shaken together, and running over. It is life that overflows the cup. It is life in the spirit of man, a noble thing, to confirm the belief that man does, indeed, bear the image of God. To win that objective will call for some losses, but they will be, for the most part, simply the loss of pride, or the loss of things which, if we arrive in heaven without them, won't be missed at all.

21

It Isn't Dirty to Be Thirty

Youth reminds us that this world of which we grow so wary, is a loved world, and that those who know and serve it best are those who love it most, not those who are afraid of it or alienated from it. Youth will just not believe that things must stay as they are. Therefore youth is always anti-establishment, as Jesus was, because every establishment is built on foundations that are partially evil and committed to keeping things as they are. If a young man does not rebel against the hypocrisy he sees in his elders, he will never grow up to recognize his own hypocrisy. If a young man doesn't seek to reform the unjust order his elders have made, he will never be able to acknowledge the injustice in the order he makes. As someone said, there's something wrong with a man who isn't a socialist before he's twenty, and who remains one after he's forty.

ROBERT I. RAINES

LUKE, in describing the beginning of Jesus' public ministry, says He was about thirty years old. We assume this is correct, even though in a conversation with the Pharisees (reported by John) Jesus is challenged by one of them after he has spoken about Abraham as his contemporary. The Jews protested, "You are not yet fifty years old, and have you seen Abraham?" This reference does not negate the view that Jesus was approximately thirty years of age when he was baptized at the river Jordan, but it does hint he could have been somewhat older than Christian scholarship generally has assumed. We can pinpoint when he was born by the reign of Augustus. We have the story of his trip to the Temple at twelve and then eighteen years of silence.

Thirty seems to be a special age. It is the age at which a man or woman becomes qualified for the United States Senate. It is the age at which a surgeon becomes eligible to be a Fellow in the American College. It is the age at which David became King of Israel.

In a way, it is the end of youth, though to be young at heart is to be forever young. In the thinking of a lot of younger people today, thirty marks the beginning of death. If you've had anything to do with journalism you know that "30" means the end.

I don't know who chose thirty as a borderline—a set of customs through which men pass from flexibility and idealism and indignation into another country in which they tend to become satisfied, fat and no longer angry—but it's a good choice. Everyone by now has heard the half-serious, half-jesting cry, "Don't trust anyone over thirty." A young theologian has written a book entitled *Don't Trust A God Over Thirty*. *Time* magazine turned the question around and asked, in the wake of widespread campus disorders, half seriously, half justingly, "Can you trust anyone under thirty?"

What are the advantages of being young, under thirty? What advantages accrue to people as the people as the result of being around for awhile and watching two or more generations of life pass?

God intends youth and age to complement each other, to reinforce each other, but what has happened is war. The gulf is widening and is poorly defined. Dean Wilbur Hinz of Northwestern University says if Booth Tarkington were writing *Seventeen* today he would call it *Eleven*. I argue there is a qualitative difference in the comparison, but there is little consensus here. No one disputes that youths are older in their understanding, while older people are becoming younger. In this sense the gap narrows and the friction builds.

In spite of profound national stress—perhaps because of it—it is a great time to be alive. It is a great time to be nineteen, and not bad being forty-nine, either. It is a dynamic age. If it is an age of anxiety, it is also an age of wonder. If it is an age of revolution, it is also an age for flying among the stars.

One advantage of being over thirty is perspective. The longer we live, the broader basis we have for comparing and seeing the size and tentativeness of life. Mere longevity, though, guarantees nothing. A school supervisor was speaking with a teacher about the improvement of her classroom styles. The teacher became incensed by the supervisor's criticism and said, "I'll have you know, sir, I've had twelve years of teaching experience!" The supervisor corrected her. "That's not true," he said, "You've had one year of experience—eleven years of repetition." Methuselah lived more than nine hundred years, but is remembered for nothing else. Jesus was dead at thirty-three and the world is still haunted by his name.

Perspective is not something on sale for one dollar and ninety-eight cents at the market, nor is it acquired merely by reading history. Knowledge of history will help, but there's no shortcut to perspective any more than there is for the clerk who wants to own the bank.

Though we've heard it over and over, Mark Twain's comment about his father remains a profound parable. Mark Twain said that when he was eighteen, his father impressed him as being stupid. "But," said the Hannibal author, "when I got to be twenty-one, I was amazed at what the old man had learned in three years."

Perspective is seeing something in its overall dimensions. It is looking at the San Fernando Valley from Mulholland Drive. It is backing off and looking from a distance. It is seeing one thing in relationship to another thing, the forest as well as individual trees.

We frequently goof because we lack this larger awareness. We say, "If I had it to do over again . . . ."

In a personal interview Mae West is quoted as saying that she can recall no mistakes; that, if she had the chance to live her life over again, she would do it all the same, but with more zing. Most of us have more regrets than that. Many would like to be able to go back and rewrite at least a couple of paragraphs.

I would like to be able to go back and tell my mother how pretty that little bedroom suite was she purchased and had brought home from an auction sale. I remember how she took me into the bedroom and showed it to me. She was so excited about her purchase, but I only shrugged.

I would like a chance to talk to Johnnie Lewis again. The Lewises, a mother and four sons, were our next-door neighbors—

one of the few black families in town, and as many such families seemed to be, fatherless. Johnnie was smart. He even wrote a couple of letters to the editor of the *Atlantic News-Telegraph*. He was killed in an automobile accident halfway through college. He died too early for the Martin Luther King dream, but he had it just the same. I wish I had listened to him more, and helped him more.

I'd like to thank my dad one more time for what he meant to me, especially for the way he treated me that afternoon when I went fishing without permission and forgot the time. He came walking through the heavy dusk after me and found me sitting there on the bank of Troublesome Creek. My pal, Denny, got a beating from his father. I got an explanation.

I'd like to undo a couple of lies, revise several little things I remember happening on the other side of thirty, but perspective can't be rushed.

Some churchmen were discussing what is the most significant and helpful way in which the church can contribute to people's lives. They observed that thousands of experts are working away at human problems. Persons in the architectural sciences and in government are at work seeking ways to renew our cities and get millions out of slums. Educators, they realized, try to prepare persons to live creatively, productively and peacefully together in the modern world. Medical men and women grapple with disease and the mystery of the unconscious. Artists dance, draw, play and compose to lift life up. These leaders asked themselves, What does the church have to supply to people's lives, to society, which is urgent, and good, and not to be found elsewhere?

One said, "It's the Spirit of God, the spirit of truth and justice, raising questions in our midst."

"The church helps men to set all things, even the commonest things, in some sort of eternal dimension," said another.

Said a third, "We are meant to be a community of love; we are that special fellowship within which all men can find acceptance and encouragement, irrespective of merit. Everywhere else you have to prove yourself first."

Much of present society has little good to say for the church— in terms of what it does for them, or to them. This is still what human beings are hungry for—a way to put the cataclysmic events and moral dilemmas of our time in perspective. While we are all part of these times, we are part of a greater show, too.

We are not the only people who have fretted over their Berkeleys or Atlantas, or had their brains shot out on battlefields at age twenty-two, or been poor, or been prejudiced against people we did not know or understand. Today our problems have somewhat specialized names, but most of them are history's old friends— war, poverty, riots, thwarted opportunities, racial fears, the stewardship of strength, violence and vulgarity, murder, arson, thievery, addiction, militarism, hunger, pollution, bribery, unemployment and disease. The noun *crisis* is not exaggerated. The Chinese word for crisis is formed by putting two smaller characters together, one meaning danger, the other opportunity.

We are riding through a storm. The church as advocate is obligated to throw its weight upon the side of the oppressed, the wounded, the ignored, because the battle for strong bodies, healthy minds, freedom and wholeness is spelled out in its orders. The church has another gift too. Within the crossfire and the despair, the hate and social failure, it can remind men on all sides of all questions that God and goodness are "from everlasting to everlasting." We are one generation, not all generations. The church can remind the human family that love and gratitude and faithfulness are not going out of style. The gospel will keep us from either underestimating or overestimating our part of the story of earth, and will keep us from taking either our success or failures as final.

The long view can be helpful. It is not so quickly panicked nor discouraged. There are advantages to being over thirty, just as there are some to being over seventy.

There's a problem in becoming thirty and we might as well face up to it. Dorothy Parker wrote about it in a poem she called "The Veteran."

> When I was young and bold and strong,
> Oh, right was right, and wrong was wrong!
> My plume on high, my flag unfurled,
> I rode away to right the world.

"Come out, you dogs, and fight!" said I,
And wept there was but once to die.

But I am old; and good and bad
Are woven in a crazy plaid.
I sit and say, "The world is so;
And he is wise who lets it go.
A battle lost, a battle won—
The difference is small, my son."

Inertia rides and riddles me;
The which is called Philosophy.

The trouble with turning thirty is that we begin to turn in our swords and we stop asking questions. We become reconciled to the world's corruption and distress and we assign it a new name, patience.

Paul, writing to Timothy, said, "Let no one despise your youth, but set the believers an example. . . ." Young people are smart enough to know that if they can't turn the corner by age thirty, they won't turn it. Something in them will expire.

Today they are raising many questions and most of them are worth asking. They are making charges of hypocrisy and most of them are true. They ask questions that plunge to the heart of the purpose of life. Many of their questions are embarrassing. They ask why, when Americans kill, it's always in the defense of decency and freedom, but when others do it, it's moral outrage. They ask why the hang-up with interracial marriage, while their predecessors stumble around and pretend there's some kind of logical or scientific validity in the way they feel. They question a preoccupation with material prosperity, and the feeling that an organ produces music more sacred than a drum. They call us uptight—a threatened, narrow-gauge people—and wave flowers in our faces to make us angry.

We've all been brought up on Tootle, the children's tale in which baby locomotives are told to stay on the tracks no matter what; don't go off to look at the buttercups, don't take short cuts to race with the stallions. The struggle is for each

135

man to live up to his own conscience, even if it is under continual pressure to go to sleep. The whole world is being divided into those that are participating in the waking up and those that would massage and tranquilize.

DAVID SHAPIRO

There is a fresh wind that blows through words like David's, but there is also a totalitarian stench in the student movement. Some students give the impression that they do not believe in the great debate at all. They prefer the bullwhip of power, and weapons of intimidation. They don't want to *challenge* the other side; they want to *paralyze* it. Faith in God is capable of withstanding all the cross-examination we can throw at it. Truth is like that, but the process must be protected. If the process goes, all goes. Within a framework of law, men can fight what they don't like, labor and disagree. They can win or lose and age makes no difference.

We need to accept ourselves where we are and make use of whatever advantages we have. The Christian gospel addresses men whether they are eighteen or eighty. It tells them they belong to each other. Jesus is the same today, yesterday and forever. His teachings and claims have to do with both the short view and the long pull. They warn us against despising either age or youth.

Genuine manhood has no tag on it, and for those, who like to think of themselves as the friends of God, thirtieth birthdays don't call for any special kind of cakes.

22

How to Keep from Going Crazy

Strike a balance between work and play—between seriousness
    and laughter. Go to church regularly, also to the ball game.
Stick with the truth even if it makes you look or feel bad.
Falsehoods are like wandering ghosts.

Forgive your enemies as part of the price you pay for the privilege of being forgiven. Realize that you are sometimes a pain in the neck yourself.

Walk. Get lots of air and sunshine, and occasionally some rain or snow in your face; some dirt on your hands.

Talk your troubles and mistakes over with someone you trust and your dreams, too.

Don't underestimate the ability of God to straighten out a situation even when you can't, and give Him a little time.

Discriminate among your fears. Learn to tell which ones are useful, which ones destructive.

Remember that the ultimate death rate is still 100 percent. You would be getting gypped if everyone got to die and you didn't.

When you can't sleep, say, "Aha! Here's a chance for a little privacy and creative thinking. All day I've been too busy to pray, now I can get around to thanking God."

Fall in love with life—with children, older people, sports cars, the theatre, music, books, cities, hills, the sea, the Bible; everything except money.

A MAN DRIVING along the Watterson Expressway had a flat tire. In the emergency lane, he jacked up the rear of the car and, with his tools, removed the lugs, took off the wheel, and mounted the spare. When he got ready to secure it, he found that his lugs had dropped into a drain opening. It was impossible to retrieve them. He knew there was no way he could drive his car without the wheel being fastened solidly to the axle. Here was a deeply grooved extra tire he had been hauling around for just such an emergency. Now that it had arrived, he still was helpless.

Sitting on a grassy bank besides his car, waiting for a tow truck, he mused on his bad luck. After awhile, from behind a fence which bordered the freeway, a stranger appeared and inquired about his problem. When he explained his trouble, the man behind the fence said, "That's not hard. Why don't you borrow one lug from each of the other three wheels? That should hold the spare on 'til you can reach the next town. At a garage, you can replace the ones you lost."

"What a good idea!" said the man with the flat tire. "That's exactly what I'll do."

By this time he realized that the fence, from behind which the man spoke, enclosed the grounds of an institution for treating the mentally ill. So he said to the man who had just supplied the ingenious advice, "Why are you in this hospital when you could think of that, and I couldn't?"

"I may be crazy," he grinned, "but I'm not stupid."

Jesus once healed a man who was accused by his contemporaries of being possessed of demons or evil spirits—of being crazy. Mark says he was a pathetic figure who kept away from society, cut himself with stones, walked naked through the streets and made strange, animal sounds. Few lines of the New Testament shine with more beauty or hope than the one which describes his appearance following his encounter with Jesus. When they heard of the miracle, the Gerasene villagers came and saw him "sitting at the feet of Jesus, clothed, and in his right mind."

Acquiring mental peace is every man's problem. Psychosis or severe neurosis is the extreme state of some; but to achieve more stability, in a stressful, topsy-turvey, ambiguity-ridden age is the problem of all.

We may not be stupid, but we are all a little crazy.

That's not altogether bad. Life was not intended to be 100 percent sensible. It would be dull if it were. People in love are slightly crazy. Politics are crazy. Fashion is crazy.

The key to *crazy* is in the inclusion of the letter *z*. It imparts the idea of zig-zagging motion, like the buzzing of a bee. *Analyze* refers to alternate movements of the intellect. We all swim round in the champagne of change, and ride merry-go-rounds of revolution, attempting to find the secret of victories in a wacky, wobbly world.

Good mental attitudes in Omaha or Oklahoma City are the result of healthy inputs. They aren't something we are born with, any more than merited happiness is a stroke of fortune—nor do we become disoriented or depressed in a single moment of time. Breakdown is the result of factors at work over longer periods. If there are disintegrative forces which eat away at our insides without our being aware of them, there are also other freeing,

138

stabilizing forces of renewal which have the power to work with the same silent effectiveness, day after day, year after year, to enable our minds to achieve wholeness and strength. The challenge is to recognize what these are and how to take advantage of them.

Reaction patterns which offer the greatest hazards to mental health are those of intense fear or anxiety, withdrawal from others and retreat into fantasy, outsized feelings of guilt or shame (from whatever source derived), and prolonged hostility expressed through undue aggression or converted into neurotic symptoms. We all share these tendencies to some extent and we must find ways to deal with them. Happiness is not the absence of problems but knowledge of how to cope with them so that they do not cripple us.

The church, with its message of forgiveness and love, its philosophy of human worth, its life of worship, prayer and acceptance, its call to embrace one another, is no luxury at all—no silly weekend hobby for the religiously inclined. Man is capable of both disorder and order, slavery and freedom. He selects which road he will follow by how seriously he takes his relationship with God, and what realities he chooses.

One thing we must learn, if we are to achieve this kind of health, is to learn how to deal with our own history. Guilt feelings have usefulness in the same way normal fear has. Both are warning systems. Criminals can steal and kill without feeling guilt or remorse, but we do not aspire toward that kind of conditioning. As long as we admit to being responsible human beings we have the problem of guilt on our hands.

When we have no way to relieve the feelings of failure we do a number of things.

We suffer. We divert our mental energies from more positive pursuits and obstruct the path of new experience. A garbage-gathering experience begins.

In worship there is usually an event which takes forty-five seconds, but which, in some ways, is more important than the lesson or sermon. It is the "Declaration of Pardon." It is meant to focus thought upon the fact that God does forgive mistakes, and He releases us from the past in that moment.

Pardon, like other New Testament terms, is borrowed from the

139

courtroom, but leaves little room for doubt as to what it means. It means freedom; it means a new start, cutting loose chains of regret.

We are bound to accept this gift of pardon, and that may be harder than it seems. It is never easy to forgive ourselves. Jesus did not teach men how to forgive themselves in six easy lessons, but He taught them about a Father's acceptance. Christianity is not the evangel of evasion, but that God accepts you, owns you, loves you, claims you for Himself—whoever you are, whatever you are, wherever you are. If He accepts you, you have no choice; you must accept yourself. You must! The alternative is self-hatred, suicide, and mental death. Self-acceptance and self-criticism are not mutually exclusive. We do not give up one in favor of the other. There is room and demand for both. Pardon is something we must learn to receive—a gift expressed in words such as these "Go your way, your faith has made you well," "Go in freedom," or "Now go and live as forgiven men."

To pardon, add perspective. Faith enables men to put things where they belong, to recognize and distinguish between those things which matter greatly and those which matter not at all.

I once wrote to my mother asking her advice about a move that would take me from one part of the country to another. She answered with wisdom, "It doesn't matter where you are, only what you are."

A basketball player quit the team. The UCLA coach was the kind of man who, to use his own words "cared about Edgar." Because Coach John Wooden was older and had seen hundreds of young athletes come and go, win and lose, develop and withdraw, he knew the young man's decision, whether justified or not, could not help but be damaging to his future. The team was large and talented, but Wooden remained as much concerned about what happened to one man as he was about the national title. His human perspective was as excellent as his knowledge of the full-court press.

Perspective is another piece of the freedom formula. Pardon is freedom from the regret and irrecoverable past. Perspective is freedom from the tyranny of any isolated moment. "Leadership," said Robert Kennedy in a political speech, "is the ability to make decisions, then to go on living with their consequences. . . ." Leadership, and faith, too, involves the ability to protect yourself against being defeated by one adversity, or becoming egotistical over one success.

Lincoln's greatness was derived partly from his ability to maintain perspective when the nation was distraught. We still search for the quality.

Good mental health is characterized by the habit of looking at people and situations in terms of their possibilities, and examining them in positive rather than negative terms. The church is where men are encouraged to do that—to love, to listen, to affirm. A small boy in Memphis was trying to describe to his mother a large building he had discovered in the neighborhood, where the door wasn't even locked, where there were tall, tall ceilings and where someone had put a big plus sign down in front. The church often forgets this and devotes its time to crying *no*.

A Christian is not called to shut his eyes to evil or to black out human pain by cerebral tricks. He is called to a life of triumph and away from self-pity. He is called to think in terms of what is yet possible. Even when his house of happiness lies in ruins, life is not without the potential of the Kingdom.

Here sits a man in his right mind, and wearing his clothes. In his face there is calmness where once fear was in charge. His crying has stopped, and the lacerations in his body are starting to heal. The townspeople stare. How can this be? They begin to think about their own lack of peace, their unrelieved guilt and lack of joy, their embattled family relationships, their fears, their inability to know who they are or to pronounce God's name.

Our minds are like great unexplored countries. The conscious and the unconscious play upon and shape each other. We cannot always make our minds do what we want them to, but we can love them as gifts and nurture them as holy possessions, knowing that by a mystery too large to explain, they are more than computers—a miracle wherein we meet God and imagine heaven.

"Create in me a clean heart, O God, and put a new and right spirit within me" is a prayer that will be in the world long after our present cities are dust. It is a prayer we can begin to implement during the next five minutes.

23

I Was in the Most Wonderful Accident

There is no health in you, Mr. Mountjoy. You do not believe
in anything enough to suffer for it or be glad. There is no
point at which something has knocked on your door and taken
possession of you. You possess yourself. Intellectual ideas,
even the idea of loyalty to your country sits on you loosely.
You wait in a dusty waiting room on no particular line
for no particular train.

WILLIAM GOLDING

A WORD WHICH did not appear in most dictionaries until recently
is *serendipity*. Its origin was in a Persian fairytale and Horace
Walpole used in *The Three Princes of Serendip*. The heroes were
gallant young men who were continually finding valuable articles
by chance.

It describes happenings which begin as mistakes or accidents,
and which, by the strange workings of Providence and circumstances, are suddenly recognized as strokes of brilliance, perhaps
as the best thing that could have happened.

A third of Genesis is devoted to the story of Joseph, a story
of serendipity.

The Joseph we meet in the New Testament is a different sort
of man—plain, humble. He is a blue collar worker who probably
never gave a public speech in his life, but knew all kinds of things
to do with wood. Joseph, in the Old Testament, is the great-
grandson of Abraham and begins life as a petted child. He
and Benjamin are the only two children of a union between Jacob
and Rachel, whom Jacob passionately loved. She died in childbirth at the time Benjamin was born. There were twelve sons, and

142

a majority of them despised Joseph because of his vision of personal superiority, and because of the father's favoritism evidenced by the coat of many colors.

Jealousy made the brothers plot to kill Joseph, but Reuben talked them out of it. He suggested they put him into a pit and leave him there, thinking he would come secretly and rescue Joseph later. This they did; then they took the repulsive robe, dipped it in goat's blood, and took it home to their father with the lie that Joseph had been killed by wild beasts.

Joseph was rescued by a caravan before Reuben could return and was taken to Egypt. His leadership abilities were quickly recognized, and after some years he rose to a position of great personal power. In a later confrontation with the brothers (when they came to borrow grain because of famine in Palestine), the now-mellowed Joseph said to them, after a game of torment with a silver cup, something like this. "When you threw me into the pit and left me there to die, your hearts were full of evil and you meant evil, but God meant it for good. He took the malice that was in you—He took your hate and made it serve His ends."

We wish somewhere we could glimpse a little contrition on Joseph's part, too, for his own complicity in the attempted crime; but it's hard to find. What is clear, and what almost brings a lump to our throats as we read the story—even if we've read it many times before—is that Joseph breaks into tears, and embraces the brothers, hugging them in obvious forgiveness. That's a better credential than anything he could have said with words.

The Bible is a catalog of failures. Any hero we choose is apt to be a man or a woman whose fallibility is as conspicuous in the record as his or her contribution to the drama of redemption. Moses had killed another man and was living in exile at the time God called him to lead his people out of bondage. David made a mess out of things, and the prophets were not flawless.

Jesus is spoken of as perfect, but he would not have used that adjective himself. He is rather, true humanity. If He is an exception to the thesis, let it be. Call the roll of the rest and you find men, not of exemplary behavior, but who, in spite of flops and failures, develop into persons of faith and voices of hope.

We could become bogged down discussing the cross as serendipity, too. Was it an evil mistake God took and reshaped into a surgical scalpel so that the body of mankind might be healed? Was it part of the wisdom of God from the beginning?

Whichever side we are on, there is an insight on which we ought to get something approaching unanimity. It is expressed in that Kilimanjaro of the Pauline writings, Romans 8:28. "... In everything God works for good with those who love him, [with those] who are called according to his purpose." That's *Revised Standard Version. The King James Version* puts it differently, "... All things work together for good to them that love God. ..." Both translations deal with the same Greek letters and words, but scholars have never fully agreed and won't, as long as the interpretation or translation of one man's work by another man is practiced. Differences will always exist about exactness of meaning of verb forms. There is no such thing as absolute correctness. Most thoughtful students of the faith believe that the RSV, published in 1946, is closer to what Paul was trying to say here. Not "... all *things* work together for good"—murders, leukemia, freeway smashups, rapes, death by malnutrition—but that "in everything" God is there seeking to bring forth good, to cooperate with men, and to reweave the ugly wools and cottons of evil into tapestries of personal and social fulfillment.

While tragedy may carry therapeutic benefits through its power to humble us, and to teach us some of the deep meanings of the world—courage, patience, hope—it is not God-sent. Tragedy is not a whip He uses to keep us in shape. All things do not work together for good in the sense that we are supposed to fold our hands and accept the whole business as ordered from above. What the New Testament does say, and something we can believe in with great intensity, is that in everything—in every failure, in every disappointment and in every hurt—there is God's concern. There is also God's resident agony, God's love and help for those who must travel through such dark territories, and who face in them the option of yoking their love with God's love in the name of a better world.

All of us blunder and face the choice of whether our falls will mean the breaking of us, or the making of us. At times it may

144

look as if there were no choice. We just lie there wounded, embarrassed and ashamed, preferring death to anything else. Without faith we are left with the limited alternative of stoic acceptance, or bitterness and remorse.

A man who believes that in everything God is at work for good knows that he can come out of the forge a better, more complete man with larger sympathy and understanding of the God to whom his life belongs. He is a descendant of Joseph who can take even his toughest hours, his worst sufferings and most calamitous defeats, and use them as new beginnings. There is more promise in a gospel which says God is there to cooperate with us and to walk beside us in our trouble, than there is in believing that the things which befall us are divine punishments sent by God to make us miserable or wake us up. They may serve that purpose, but such logic can destroy faith's integrity, too, and that's the message of Job.

Serendipities also may involve our relationships with other people. Something goes wrong. We quarrel with a member of our family, or become alienated from someone close to us, and we are both miserable. If we choose, we can sulk and invent arguments to prove we were right and they were wrong. Where we bring to such disasters the belief that, even here, a new opportunity exists for interaction and acceptance—that in everything God is ready to cooperate for good—we have the chance of coming out on an even higher plane of love with that person than was possible before hard words drove their wedge between us.

When it comes to war and peace, again it is hard to see how God can take mistrust and anger and death, and, through such materials, release anything good into the social bloodstream, but to believe otherwise is to allow ourselves to be drowned in the swamps of atheism.

There are three options. One is that God is not involved at all in history; another is that He is involved on the side of evil; and third, that he is involved on the side of good. The first choice costs nothing. One simply shrugs his shoulders or bites his lip. The second is incongruous. The third doesn't have many takers either, even though the call of the Christ is to enter the world

145

and to fight on the side of God, believing that He's already there. God has no draft, no selective service; He has only the appeal of two pierced hands, and the joy of obedience.

In Dr. Zhivago, Boris Pasternak has the tormented physician say, "There are but two forces at work in the world . . . the cudgel and the inner music." All around us today is the sound of the cudgel—noisy, raucous, full of fury, the power of the big stick. We whose hope lies in the emancipation not the regimentation, of the human spirit put our money and our lives on the quiet power of the inner music.

Death itself is so irrevocable and final, it is hard to view it in terms of an event which can be changed into something beautiful and abiding. One example often given of serendipity is the artist who accidentally spills drops of paint on a carefully planned, almost finished canvas. Rather than try to wipe the spot clean, he takes those spilled drops and, with his brush, works them into a new shape or a new figure which joins the scene—perhaps even turns out to be the most engaging detail or personality of all.

This is how we need to look upon death. Prayer always changes the situation, as does every man's death. After death, it often seems to us that there are no spilled drops left with which to work. That is not really so because the lives of others bear a continuing influence on us. Most of what we are is a heritage from those who preceded us.

George Matheson wrote two of our finest hymns: "O Love That Wilt Not Let Me Go," and "Make Me A Captive Lord." He also wrote a book, *Representative Men in the Bible,* in which he gives the story of Joseph a musical twist. He said Joseph's life is like a Chopin prelude. That all preludes have three parts. In the first, the melody is free and unrestrained. In the second, it moves through tangled places, impeded on its way by the intervention of resistant elements. In the third, the melody comes out into the open once more; the tangles vanish, the impediments are removed, and the notes of the first part reappear in a new connection and with new power.

Joseph's early life was like the first movement. He was goodlooking, popular, cocky, and he had the world on a yo-yo string. The second movement included the attempted murder, his sale as a slave and his first months in the Egyptian dungeon. In his own land, he was already numbered among the dead; in Egypt, he was unnumbered either among the dead or living. He was a cipher. Then came discovery, honor and finally reconciliation not only with his brothers, but even the miracle of being held once more in his father's arms.

This is what makes men saints of serendipity. Not that they have attained moral excellence, for they are accepted by God and loved by God even without it, but that they are ready to see in all of life—*all* of it—the potential of the kingdom. Crying and dying, tears and tribulations, are part of the price of God's new day and God's new community.

Dr. George Matheson concluded his study of the boy in the gay coat, who became the man weeping with happiness on the shoulders of his brothers, with this prayer.

Lord, teach me the power of life's seeming arrests! Often have I felt the grief of Joseph. Often have the bright dreams of youth appeared to fade, and the shadows of the prison house to close over the growing man. I have cried in the bitterness of my soul. "The promise of the morning is broken; I shall never now find the treasure for which I have sought so long!" And lo, I have found it in the prison house, in the dungeon, in a panel of the locked door. I had sought it in all likely places— in the fields, in the woods, in the homes of the rich and mighty; and it has come to me in the one spot where its presence seemed impossible. Thou has answered me as Thou answeredest Job—"out of the whirlwind." I had been looking to all calm places for an answer. I had looked to the gentle dawn; I had gazed on the roseate morning; I had stood in the pensive twilight; I had communed with the still and starry night; I had listened upon my bed when the pulse of life beat low. From none of these did my answer come. Then the whirlwind swept by, and I said, "There will be Divine silence now; I cannot hope for Thy voice anymore!" And behold it was from the whirlwind that Thy voice *came!* What earth's silence could not give, what earth's zephyrs could not give was given by the storm! Let me never again fear the shut gate; let me never more dread the interrupted journey! Teach me that my Calvary may be my crown! Tell me that my Patmos may be my promotion! Show me that my Damascus darkness may be my dazzling daylight! Reveal to me that there may be progress through life's pauses, voices in life's valley; symmetry in life's sighs, music in life's maladies, beauty in life's burdens, work in life's wilderness. Then shall I know why this portrait has been placed in the great gallery of deathless souls.   Amen

24

The Name of the Game Is Man

Being human is a surprise, a flash of light, a moment in time rather than a thing in space.

ABRAHAM HESCHEL

LIKE TARZAN swinging his way through the jungle, Americans jump from one cliché to another. Clichés serve two purposes: they keep us from becoming too tense, and they offer oblique glimpses of the truth in the same way poetry does.

One which seems as if it will be around for awhile is *the name of the game*.

It indicates a question, What is the purpose of whatever we are talking about?

In each activity of life there is an objective, or a controlling aim, which in most cases can be reduced to a single word.

In politics it is to get elected, to take over the seat of power. There is usually a frosting. Arguments that one's motives are pure, that one longs to serve his people, to solve the nation's problems and to get the country moving again are presented by candidates; but the nitty-gritty of politics is to win at the ballot box.

148

In business the name is profit. Business men serve the common good, and there is satisfaction in serving the public; but the motivation is unanimous—it is spelled profit.

Among artists and musicians and amateur athletes the name of the game is excellence.

In religion it is grasping hold of the meaning of life.

Two questions that deserve answers are what is the purpose of my life, and what is the purpose of history.

If our lives have meaning, history does, too. Or, we may reverse the order and say that if life as a whole is meaningful, our own lives participate in that significance. Maybe its *one* question.

Oriental minds seem to be able to separate them. The Hindu can say that even if history is incomprehensible, man still has a soul, and whether life on earth makes sense or not, the soul is eternal.

Occidentals find it hard to agree. The western mind is so wrapped up in history's outcome that the world's life, and the life of the individual, stand or fall together.

What is life's purpose? It's hard to imagine an older question—unless that might be What are we having for supper? What's it all about? Life is an endless search for the answer. It runs through literature like a spinal cord. It stands permanent watch at the center of our brain.

Early in life, we are inclined to answer the question by agreeing that the purpose of life is to be happy. This begs the question. It simply begets a new one, a definition of happiness. It's not much of an answer, but about the only answer many people could give. To be happy? Happiness is not only a thin explanation for life, it even includes the risk of being wrong.

Another answer, worn smooth by centuries of handling, is pleasure—to find enjoyment in living. In John Updike's *Couples* various husband-wife combinations attempt to find their kicks in daring extra-marital adventures. Says Updike, in a review, "It's a happy-ending book—everybody gets what he wants. The kicker, of course, is that getting it is just as frustrating as not getting it, and the would-be Hedonists retreat in defeat from their obsessive adulteries."

149

Jesus tells about a rich man whose crops were so extensive he had to erect new barns in order to store them. His purpose was to be safe. It was to achieve independence, so that under no circumstances would he ever be forced to reach out for the mercy and the assistance of another human being. His stainless-steel security turned out to be a house filled with loneliness. The words of Jesus ring down into our own age—into our poverty and affluence alike. ". . . A man's life does not consist in the abundance of his possessions" (Luke 12:15). A man who lays up treasure for himself but is not rich toward God is a fool; he is a man who has misread the purpose of life. He has the name of the game misspelled.

Another answer more acceptable to our own time sounds like this: the purpose of life is to do good in the world and to help others. It is hard to argue against this raison d'être. Implied in the parable of the rich man and his barns is the idea that if he had a broader compassion, he could have found plenty of incidents of hunger and need to solve his storage problems. Christianity is the servant life. We love God through our neighbor. Those disfranchised, poor, homeless and jobless are our concern. We are in the world to bear each other's burdens and thus ". . . fulfill the law of Christ."

We can hardly say that this is the end of the search. The name of the game is not simply to have enough of everything. Find someone who has everything he wants in life and you will find misery. We must align ourselves with the goal of bringing a better life to all men—not only fair employment, but full employment; not only fair education and fair housing, but full education and full housing. At the same time, we are foolish to imagine that once we *all* have *all* those things, we have found the purpose of life. If material comfort is of itself an inadequate purpose for us, how can it be the ultimate aim of life simply to give more of it to others? Donald Baille is right when he asks

And if we haven't really found a big enough purpose to be the end and object of life for ourselves, how can we solve the problem by getting busy in the service of others? We don't know how to serve them. We don't know what we want to

150

give them. It would be just going round and round in a circle chasing our tails because we don't know what it's all about.

Another answer comes not from the Bible nor from the church, but out of the agony of modern life.

An increasing number of sensitive and perceptive writers today give this answer: the purpose of life is to be human. It is to be a man, a total man.

Jewish scholar Abraham Heschel says it most often and best.

I am born a human being; what I have to acquire is being human. The tragedy is that our way of thinking and living leads to a gradual liquidation of the riches of the inner man. We are losing any understanding of the meaning of being human. . . . The truth of being human is gratitude, the secret of existence is appreciation, its significance is revealed in reciprocity. Mankind will not die for lack of information; it may perish for lack of appreciation. . . . Being human is a surprise, a flash of light; a moment in time rather than a thing in space.

Heschel illustrates the thesis with a cute story.

A baby was born in the hospital, and the father's first chance to see his firstborn child was after it was brought home and placed in the crib. His friends saw how he leaned over the crib and an expression of extreme bewilderment was in his face. Why do you look so bewildered? Impossible, he answered, how can they make such a fine crib for $29.50?

The contention of both Judaism and Christianity is that man cannot be human, satisfyingly human and intendedly human, without a relationship with God. The Westminister Catechism put it this way, "The chief end of man is to glorify God and enjoy Him forever." Man cannot be human alone—without God, or without his neighbor. Daily we help to create each other as persons, and we also are created and formed out of our relationship, or lack of relationship with God. The purpose of life is to find ourselves and to free ourselves within His purpose. No other answer will satisfy. This is the name of the game which underlies all our other interests in happiness, security, achievement and feelings of self-worth.

This becomes the basis for an answer to the second question, What is the purpose of history? Biblical man sees God at work in history. He understands God in terms of two convictions. One, God loves him. Second, God is faithful; He keeps His promises. Beyond these cardinal affirmations, theology fans out in a thousand directions.

History's purpose is God's purpose, and His purpose is to mold man in His own image, to distill some invisible beauty. It is a beauty which involves persons and their relationship with each other. It involves us as persons of independent value, and it involves us in community. We cannot pull those propositions neatly apart, because our success or failure to live as children of one Father reveals what we are more than anything we might say.

We live in the midst of many revolutions. Two of the most obvious ones are technological dislocation and black revolution. Both bring pain, trauma, uncertainty and bitterness. Both also contain the wheat of redemption. They demand radical reassessments. They expose the truth that we may have it made in terms of the houses we live in, the clothes we wear, the cars we drive, the colleges from which we have been graduated, the elegance of our friends and still not have it made at all as human beings. Big barns on our property tell nothing about our involvement with helping to perfect His new creation. Storage sheds tell nothing about gentleness or caring.

The campaign of the poor is a political dramatization of the fact that, in spite of America's high productivity and general prosperity, there are still millions of people for whom the going is tough. That fact is hardly a matter of debate, but how to remedy it is. There are no divinely revealed answers on how to conquer poverty. There is a divinely revealed imperative to care and to be more anxious about people than barns.

The survival of the United States is important to God as well as to the United States. Still, survival is not the name of the game. We have a better chance of surviving if survival is not our national primary concern. The concern must be with the quality of our corporate life, our honest-to-God acceptance of responsibility for each other and our desire to become both the men and the commonwealth to which God is calling us.

I refuse to believe that the best we can hope for is an armed truce. We must work not for a peace of equilibrium but for genuine mutuality. Black power balanced against white power; and students against the Establishment are conditions to be remedied. It is not enough that Jew, Catholic and Protestant speak softly but wear brass knuckles of suspicion while jealousy hides inside velvet gloves of ecumenical politeness. The lightning, wind and hail of revolution spell option. We can pull down the shades, bar the windows, go to bed and pull up the covers, waiting for the storm to pass. Or, we can go out bravely into the darkness with a lantern in our hand.

V
HOPE IS A SKYLINE

25

America to God: Please Come Back, All Is Forgiven

In our complex urban society the powers of the spirit seem to be very slight when measured against the mighty forces of modern life. Indeed, the church itself seems frail, almost fragile, in comparison with the vast organizations and stupendous forces of the secular world. The church is physically overshadowed by the skyscrapers of our cities. It seems to exist by sufferance of the surrounding community.

But the truth is just the opposite. This surrounding society, with its vast complexities and fantastic forces, exists by sufferance of the community of faith. Only because of the covenants men make with one another and with their God—the trusts to which they pledge themselves and which they keep—can our society exist at all.

It has been said that no one ever planned the skyline of a great city. That skyline is the product of all sorts of uninspired and functional efforts, produced without any thought of their total effect.

But when seen from a little distance it becomes a whole. You have seen it as you have approached New York from across the river, or Chicago from the lakefront, or San Francisco from across the bay—especially at evening. Then all these results of practical building become a totality. The rigid angularities of individual structures of steel and concrete are blended into a single silhouette—flowing, romantic, beautiful in its wholeness.

It is so in the life of the city—and in the life of the church in the city. If we build as well as we know, we shall build better than we know. For God himself becomes a participant in the enterprise. By his grace the results of our separate efforts and separate faithfulnesses become parts of a mighty whole—the skyline of an Eternal City, a "city which has foundations, whose builder and maker is God!"

TRUMAN B. DOUGLASS

IN SPITE of an impressive array of cities, especially newer cities like Houston, Phoenix and San Diego, America is not the world. The world is now a village and America only a neighborhood. There may have been a time when, like the monarch of Siam, Americans would have drawn the United States on the map very large and the rest of the world very tiny, but our perspective has cleared. Today we are trying to find the right mixture of great power and responsible partnership.

Nevertheless, much of the world's hopes depend upon this young land's ability to weather her own heavy seas, and in the process prove that freedom and justice for many are more durable realities than regimentation by a few.

Today, the call is out for men of wisdom, men of leadership and character who can point the way for the renewal of the American society, and through it, the renewal of the hopes of all civilized peoples.

Dean Rusk, former Secretary of State, has said, "The survival of man is in the hands of men." This is no sub-Christian remark. God always worked through men, not around them.

If we use Paul's formula from the letter to the Romans that ". . . suffering produces endurance, endurance produces character, and character produces hope," we first have to take hold of a scarlet thread. These are days of suffering for America. There is anguish in the land. We revel in a gross national product which approaches the trillion mark, but are more fearful about what is happening to the American experiment than we have been at any time since those first tough settlers camped on Virginia shores. As violence and division grow, we wonder if we may not be going down the drain, a victim of suicide.

We need look back no farther than John Glenn's first orbital flight to realize that there has been, since then, a shattering of the American spirit. Do you remember how we laughed at that scene in the New Concord gym when Colonel Glenn returned to be honored by the townspeople among whom he had grown up? How proud we were! Admittedly, this has its hopeful side. A fire alarm system often involves smashing a small glass shield in order to get at the button that will bring help. The glass that littered the early morning streets of Newark, Rochester, Cleveland and Detroit in the middle sixties represented national illusions which deserved to be shattered by bricks. Unity built America, and the death of our mysterious oneness—a oneness that included diversity from the start—may signal an end to the story as frightening as the Kennedy and King killings.

If those who represent the Establishment are often sick inside, and scared about what is happening to the national spirit, many other Americans (especially the one-hundred million born since the end of World War II), rejoice in what looks to them like the beginning of a better day—a time characterized by more exposure of hypocrisy, more freedom from conformity and a less dollarized conception of what it means to be a successful human being. Whether these are good times or bad times may depend upon where we sit.

The late sixties were years marked by a special degree of misery. Viet Nam and domestic violence became the new sharp synonyms of pain, but pain has always been the price of growth. It is nothing new to the community of the cross.

A man who earned the right to call himself an Apostle wrote

. . . as servants of God we commend ourselves in every way: through great endurance in afflictions, hardships, calamities, beatings, imprisonments, tumults, labors, watching, hunger; by purity, knowledge, forbearance, kindness, the Holy Spirit, genuine love, truthful speech, and the power of God; with the weapons of righteousness for the right hand and for the left; in honor and dishonor, in ill repute and good repute. We are treated as imposters, and yet are true; as unknown, and yet well known; as dying, and behold we live, as punished, and yet not killed; as sorrowful, yet always rejoicing;

159

as poor, yet making many rich; as having nothing, and yet possessing everything (II Corinthians 6:4-10 RSV).

America was built out of such material. More than fifty percent of the Mayflower arrivals did not survive the first winter, and the power to endure was the beginning of a story of remarkable strength. Plants are not made rugged in hot houses but in the presence of wind, rain and heavy snow.

> The cry of man's anguish went up to God,
> Lord, take away pain!
> The shadow that darkens the world Thou has made;
> The close coiling chain
> That strangles the heart: the burden that weighs
> On the wings that would soar—
> Lord, take away pain from the world Thou hast made
> That it love Thee the more!
> Then answered the Lord to the cry of the world,
> "Shall I take away pain,
> And with it the power of the soul to endure,
> Made strong by the strain?
> Shall I take away pity that knits heart to heart,
> And sacrifice high?
> Will ye lose all your heroes that lift from the fire
> White brows to the sky?
> Shall I take away love that redeems with a price,
> And smiles with its loss?
> Can ye spare from your lives that would cling unto Mine
> The Christ on His cross?"
>
> AUTHOR UNKNOWN

We are a young people. A foreign observer recently called us "the short-distance crusader nation," but we will disprove that.

Endurance, though, is not quite enough. If it is to result in character, it must be directed toward a goal. Character requires a referent. Life cannot be measured simply against itself. There must be some magnetic north against which the compass is adjusted.

Today many people want nothing to do with the church. They

are bored with it. Their world is the world of car payments, the beach, the boss and the bed. Men have to find greater things to live for than their own comfort, or they go crazy. The task is to make human life human, but we can only know what is human if we have a reality with which to compare and test.

John Gardner, outstanding American citizen and active in public affairs, nails this truth by writing,

> The reason Americans have not trapped the bluebird of happiness, despite the most frantic efforts the world has ever seen, is that happiness as total gratification is not a state to which man can aspire. The irony is that we should have brought such unprecedented dynamism to the search for such a static condition.
>
> It might be possible for an impoverished nation to harbor the delusion that happiness is simply comfort and pleasure and having enough of everything. But we have tried it, and we know better.

If we grant the accuracy of this statement, we must ask, To what state can we properly aspire without becoming disappointed fools? It is to be the men God meant us to be. It is to be a man. For this purpose the gospel has come.

Character not only needs a reference; it must also find its verification in human relationships. If the national character is in danger today, it is at the point of the quality of these relationships that it can be faulted most readily. National character is personal character written large, and personal character is made up from the way a man relates to other men—to his employees or employer, to his neighbor, his wife, his children, his government and those who are different from himself.

Improvement in our public character will depend upon the ability to improve the quality of human relationships. Rights are part of the challenge, but they are only a piece of the larger problem. Though urban living is not fatal to friendship in depth, it is not conducive to it. If friendship fails in the race to reach twenty-thousand dollar annual incomes, then we have a case of termites and the future does not look good.

161

Poverty must be conquered. Prejudice must be destroyed. The problem of pollution must be solved. But beyond these, people must be treated as living souls. Human beings are not machines, statistics, welfare cases, bank accounts or animals. A person is a world, an end in himself, a reminder of what it is all about. At the feet of God we must seek pardon for having lost our way. In our own reconciled relationship with Him, we must experience a grace that will lead us to rediscover those around us as persons, including our nearest neighbors and the members of our own families.

Lord, come back to us. We forgive. Forgive us!

One day I ran onto a picture of myself in a scrapbook. I was about seven and I think I was wearing my first pair of long pants. I found myself looking back into the life of this little boy as a total outsider. I felt, in some ways, a complete stranger to him; still I knew this was I. Life has changed very much since then; the wheel has gone round many times. The child in the long trousers is gone in order that I might live. Without hope, without God, without faith, life has a way of slipping into nothingness. Against this reverse momentum God has given us the forward action and energy of hope.

As we are renewed in our lives and in our own characters, our nation, too, will sense a fresh flow of blood, and history will clap her hands.

26

Tomorrow's Weather: Partial Clearing

We were at work in a trench. The dawn around us; gray was the sky above; gray the snow in the pale light of dawn; gray the rags in which my fellow prisoners were clad, and gray their faces . . . I was struggling to find the reason for my sufferings, my slow dying. In a last violent protest, against the hopelessness of imminent death, I sensed my spirit piercing through the enveloping gloom. I felt it transcend that hopeless, meaningless world, and from somewhere I heard a victorious "yes" in answer to my question of the existence of an ultimate purpose. At that moment a light was lit in a distant farmhouse, which stood on the horizon as if painted there, in the midst of the miserable gray of a dawning morning in Bavaria. *"Et lux in tenebris lucet"*—and the light shineth in the darkness.

VIKTOR FRANKL

IN AN AGE of jet travel, air buses and high-speed trains (soon expected to run at speeds of 125 or 150 miles an hour), the steamship seems like an appointment with history. Still there is a persistent fascination with the sea and sailing, the deep-throated whistle of a liner leaving her berth, Long Beach's new plaything, the *Queen Mary,* or the story of Paul's shipwreck told in Acts 27.

Sometimes we get a limited image of Paul as a theologian and scholar. In Romans, for example, he takes his reader into deep intellectual water as he talks about sin and the law. In Colossians, he discusses Jesus in soaring, philosophical, cosmic terms. In Corinthians, he is the master moralist. As he teaches, tramping and battling his way across the pages of Acts, taking the gospel from its tiny provincial setting and converting it within one lifetime into a world faith, he shines as a very practical fellow, someone who would be handy to have around in a time of crisis.

The most dramatic line in the story comes when the storm had been raging for two weeks and Paul, though technically a prisoner on his way to Rome to be tried for subversion, enjoyed camaradarie with the crew. In emergencies all of life's formal fluff and nice distinctions are discarded. In this situation both Paul and the ship's complement had begun to feel that time had about run out. Things became as desperate as they could possibly get. Describing the dark prospect, Paul, in some memoranda or diary entry which eventually came into Luke's hands, wrote:

163

"Then, for many days there was no glimpse of sun or stars and we were still in the grip of the gale, all hope of our being saved was given up" (Acts 27:20 PHILLIPS).

It is in this setting that Paul emerges as a man of unconquerable faith, sure vision and practical judgment. He told the crew that his prayers to God had convinced him all would be saved. He summoned the men to a new show of courage and convinced them that their best chances lay in remaining with the ship, rather than abandoning it in favor of the lifeboats.

Soon, soundings revealed that the water was becoming shallow and land was near. The vessel seemed to be at the point of breaking apart, but Paul exhorted the sailors to hold on! Something told him that if they could last a few more hours, they could win against the weather and the waves. The seamen took Paul at his word, and then follows the magnificent entry. ". . . They let out four anchors from the stern, and prayed for day to come."

Our times have been, in a way, a kind of prolonged typhoon or an age of rage. They are best described as years of anger and fire, division, death, revolution, Armageddon and blood. The problems and pressures are near and real. We can feel. We can see. We can smell. We can hear the groans of a society in labor. We know ours, indeed, is a voyage through storm.

Once during a thunderstorm, as the bowling alleys of heaven came alive, there was the pitter-patter of small feet in our bedroom. Soon a miniature, comforted form was snuggled securely between mother and father. It reminded me how my mother would be frightened by such violence when I was a child. She would rise from bed and sit in the living room as the house shook and the lightning illuminated the inside of 208 Maple Street as in a horror movie. Also awakened by the noise, I would go and sit with her until the thunder started to weaken and the sky turned to soft sobbing in place of wild percussion.

Four anchors are dropped from the stern. What are they? Where do we turn? What do we do? Where do we seek safety and calm when life assaults our ears and frightens our hearts?

The first is *God* Himself. He is not our *last* resort but our *first*. God communicates Himself to us through prayer. There is no point in saying, "But I don't know how to pray." Prayers do not require words. They can consist of any kind of turning toward God. Silences are often eloquent enough, and, if silence is all we have to bring, it will do, provided God-ward across the mute meadows of self, there moves a love and supplication which bears our own existential endorsement.

Storms come in different styles. In the same way they descend as hurricanes, as hail, thunder, lightning, or floods, so do adversities invade our lives as sorrow, heart attacks, divorce actions, or other kinds of disappointment rack our bodies with despair.

Nationally, heavy weather has come in the form of a people divided against themselves, in the breakdown of communication and cooperation, and in the loss of confidence in the vision of "one nation under God." Politics of disruption have replaced politics of debate, and we are in trouble. We don't seem to be able to find that narrow creative corridor which divides dissent from destruction. By allowing our suburbs to become all white, and our inner cities all black, we have inherited the wind.

God is not a storm cellar, a place to hide. The church must do more than shout, "Back to God! Back to the Bible! Back to religion!"

Rather, it must inspire men to work for a larger justice for all men and for changes in themselves. There is no clearer word from God than this. There is no other road to peace.

Then they cried to the Lord in their trouble, and he delivered them from their distress; . . . he made the storm be still, and the waves of the sea were hushed. Then they were glad because they had quiet, and he brought them to their desired haven (Psalm 107:19, 29 RSV).

Another anchor is *friendship,* and often we encounter God through our friends. God is not a ghost. He is the Spirit who comes to us as mercy, calm and understanding through others.

God doesn't need to authenticate Himself by writing messages in the clouds, or historical legerdemain. He simply comes to us when we need Him, restores us when it seems as though our resources are depleted. He does this through the plainest kinds of meetings and conversations, sometimes through nothing more than a touch on the shoulder.

Emerson wrote that he didn't find his friends; God gave them to him. How can we enlarge upon that or upon these words, straight out of Galilee

> Greater love has no man than this, that a man lay down his life for his friends. You are my friends if you do what I command you. No longer do I call you servants, for the servant does not know what his master is doing; but I have called you friends, for all that I have heard from my Father, I have made known to you (John 15:13-15 RSV).

Friend may not be a very theological word, but it is full of breath and humanity. When someone we know is in the grip of a gale, it is sometimes in our power to be the bearers of the balm of Gilead. We cannot go with an answer. As a minister, I took that pressure off myself a long time ago, but we can go with ourselves. We can bear love in our hands and that is to bear God. What we cannot endure alone we can endure together.

Dr. Francis Pritchard has described growing up in Texas. He says that when blizzards roar across the plains in winter, the cattle huddle tightly together for warmth and protection. This is often the only way we can handle sorrow, too.

There are certain kinds of suffering we have to do alone. When a husband dies, or a wife dies, there is, during those first days or weeks the supporting affection and help of children and brothers and sisters and friends. At last one is alone with his grief and, like Jesus in Gethsemane, there is a solitary dimension to such tears that cannot and should not be avoided. Even these moments may not be as alone as they seem, for even they are affected by the radiated warmth of mankind.

A third anchor is *earth,* the breast of life itself, upon which we can lean and await the light of dawn.

Richard Hovey writes of our need.

> I have need of the sky,
> I have business with the grass,

166

I will up and get me away where the hawk is wheeling
Lone and high,
And the slow clouds go by.
I will get me away to the waters that glass
The clouds as they pass.
I will get me away to the woods.

Nature has her own special benedictions that heal and repair. Slowly despair gives way, even though we had decided she was to be our companion forever.

"By and by," says Arthur Gossip, Scottish divine, writing after the death of his wife, "the gale dies down and the moon rises and throws a lane of gold to us across the blackness and the heaving of the tumbling waters. After all it is not in the day, but in the night that star rises after star, and constellation follows constellation, and the immensity of this bewildering universe looms up before our staggered minds. But it is in the dark that the faith becomes biggest and bravest, that its wonders grow yet more and more."

As we wait for that amber highway to appear, we can continue to listen to the sea, drink from the fountain of blue-gray hills, feel rain and cold and put our faces against the bark of a tree.

The fourth anchor is the *future*.

First, our turning is to God from whom all blessings come. "But seek first his kingdom and his righteousness, and all these things shall be yours" (Matthew 6:33 RSV). Then we turn to each other, and we become real Christians to each other. We turn to that which cannot answer back, except by a twirling leaf, or fragrance, or some silent signal of foreverness and then we drop anchor number four.

We turn to tomorrow. Though when life is going badly even the smallest thought about another day is abrasive to us, this is a turning we must do. To become immobilized is to die. To look only backwards is to become insane. We must look ahead, reach ahead and begin to nourish our imaginations with all kinds of original possibilities.

We hear much about the theology of hope. And surely ours is an age tailor-made for that kind of encouragement. Hoping is different from dreaming. While it is a word about the future, it is also a powerful word about the present. It is a position one takes (based upon God's promises) which frees the present moment, liberating, exciting and imprinting it with beauty and meaning.

In *The Pilgrim's Progress,* Christian and Evangelist have a conversation near the start of their journey to the city of God. Evangelist is trying to get Christian to have some sense of direction, to have something to key on as he begins the long and difficult pilgrimage which will take him through the Slough of Despond, to the Interpreter's House, to a town called Vanity where there's a fair going on, and to Doubting Castle.

He points a finger off into the distance and asks Christian if he can see the wicket gate of the City. He looks for quite awhile, straining his eyes, and finally confesses that he cannot.

Evangelist asks, "Do you see yonder shining light?"

Christian looks again. After a few seconds, he turns to Evangelist as a smile spreads slowly over his face, and says, "I think I do."

"Keep that light in your eye. . . ." says Evangelist.

That's the gift of faith to you. No matter how violent the storm becomes, the light will not go out. It will flicker, but will not fail. Eventually, it will be replaced by the daylight Paul knew was on its way.

Tomorrow's weather: partial clearing.

27
Stop Trying So Hard!

It is a little recognized fact that every person is in debt. We never get out of debt. The only people who are paid up are in cemeteries. To live is to be indebted—to God and to man. Sleep is merely a brief, daily moratorium on our indebtedness. This does not mean that we have to live constantly under the strain of creditors pressing us. It is not necessary to become addicts of the strenuous life. Rather, calmly and confidently we need to commit ourselves to the fact that what we are, have, can acquire, or can become is not ours to use as we wish. We owe it. To be a human being is to be in debt.

DR. R. LOFTON HUDSON

DR. HUDSON'S statement could sound like bad news. In another way it is marvelous news, for most of us feel, on a fairly regular basis, the pressure of debts. We live with a secret dream that if we can just once get ourselves over the next two hurdles, life suddenly will look very good and very free. If we can junk that idea and accept the fact that we will be in debt as long as we live—that this is the problem of all men and the necessary conditions of being human—we may be able to take some new, deep breaths.

Hear Paul. ". . . It is, remember, by grace and not be achievement that you are saved. . . . He [God] shows for all time the tremendous generosity . . . toward us in Christ Jesus. It was nothing you could or did achieve—it was God's gift of grace which saved you. No one can pride himself upon earning the love of God" (Ephesians 2:5-9 PHILLIPS).

Roman Catholics have traditionally had a slightly different idea about grace. Catholic theology has understood grace as a supernatural gift of God to an intellectual creature bestowed with a view to eternal life. Man, having lost grace in the Fall, has it restored by the sacrifice of Christ. Grace is spiritual energy working upon and shaping the soul.

Generally, Protestants do not isolate the soul from the body. They do not think of the soul in separation. Instead of saying man *has* a soul, they are more inclined to say he *is* a soul and that his *total being* is the object of God's interest and love. They do not look upon the soul as having its own separate career; rather, they interpret the resurrection of the body to mean that in heaven they will have a new body, suitable for their new estate.

Grace for Protestants is an attribute of God. It means unmerited favor—something received without being deserved. Luther said what men receive is not an invisible power nor a spiritual antiseptic, but the assurance that God Himself is gracious, that He is gracious toward us.

Grace describes the basis of our relationship with God. Our relationship with God is one based upon His mercy, not upon our perfectibility. We hear, "I'm as good as all those hypocrites who go and sit in church each Sunday." We listen to them list all the good things they have done in and with their lives—"I have never cheated, I have never lied," et cetera. This misses the point, if our lives are to be lived by grace.

Grace means God loved us before we loved him. It means the Prodigal Son can come home. It is an announcement. It is why Protestants put the preaching of the Word and the receiving of the Supper on the same level. Each is part of a communicated Word about acceptance.

The fact that we cannot earn favor with God by exemplary conduct, by the money we contribute, by the prayers we say or by the kindnesses we bestow, is hard for Americans to swallow. We are enterprising, ambitious people. We have made a religion out of achievement. We live by a gospel of excellence. We are winners. We work furiously to get where we want to get. We understand the power of money and brains. We invented the cliché, "Money isn't everything, but it's way ahead of whatever's in second place." We are builders. If we see something we want, we go after it.

This is not to suggest that these are qualities for which we need apologize. Out of American drive and love of excellence have come profound blessings, not only for our own people but for millions of others.

Our style of life makes it hard for us to come up against something we cannot get merely by the expenditure of effort and ability, yet that's what the New Testament says is the case where ultimate destiny is concerned. We cannot buy it; we cannot earn it; we cannot steal it. We may only receive it and be glad.

There are a number of things we cannot earn, only accept. The Christian faith is not a set of guidelines on how to become rich, successful or to achieve peace of mind. If faith is that kind, it belongs to us rather than we belonging to it. Christianity is a special stance toward God—a relationship of trust and of openness—beyond that, getting specific is risky.

A Christian must surrender sovereignity of self. He must give up the idea that he is his own master, his own possession and that if he punches all the right buttons he will squeeze his way through to the Promised Land. He must sign a Declaration of Dependence. Until he does, he experiences bondage. It may be a subtle bondage, but the chains will be there and they will be heavy.

In a sensitivity group two persons with strong arms kneel each on one knee on a large mat and hold out their arms as catchers. Members of the group are then asked to take turns falling into the arms of these receivers. The trick is to fall, semi-rigid and eyes closed, first forward, then backward. It takes courage. The purpose of the drill is to give the faller the experience of committing himself entirely into someone else's hands. The thought of falling face down on a hard surface and winding up bloodied and injured is a fear each has to cope with and this has to be balanced by the promise of someone else that this will not happen.

Such experience is representative of the larger difficulty we have in entrusting ourselves or abandoning ourselves to anyone else or to anything. One of the closest parallels for me was the moment I held up my hand and promised to surrender my life for my country if it became necessary. This must be part of what Jesus meant when he said we must become as children if we are to enter the Kingdom. As children we quickly abandon ourselves to the wisdom and custody of our parents. We trust them. If they lead us along what looks like a dangerous path, we still accompany them because we believe in their love and protection. As we grow older, we take more and more responsibility for ourselves. What had been easy becomes increasingly difficult.

In Akron and Albuquerque, Birmingham and Bakersfield, it is possible for us to take too much responsibility for ourselves, to wind up with magnified self-sufficiency, to become tense, paranoid and incapable of either understanding or enjoying a life of Christian grace.

This is different from the tendency to push our problems off on God. There is a dependence which is yellow, weak and cowardly. Psalm 8 (KJV) tells us we are made "but little lower than the

171

angels," and that we have been assigned responsible dominion over the Creation. Faith is not throwing the burden back upon God for wars, disasters and failures, but there is a dependence which answers and interdicts our vanity and sin, a dependence best summarized in Ephesians 2:8 (PHILLIPS).

> It is, remember, by grace and not by achievement that you are saved. . . . No one can pride himself on earning the love of God.

These, I confess, are breezes of health blowing through my own problems and dreams.

Life itself is a gift. We cannot create ourselves. Forgiveness we cannot purchase. Paul Wellman, who lived in Los Angeles for a number of years before his death in 1966, wrote a novel called *The Chain*. It tells about a young man who, in a fit of temper, killed his own brother. Later, this man became an Episcopal priest, but his life never lost the torment of his terrible mistake. Critically injured in an accident some years later, he was rushed to the emergency room of a hospital; and there, to the amazement of the surgical staff, a self-imposed chain was found welded about his body. We cannot pardon ourselves even with iron crosses. We can but listen to the message of grace and know that God does forgive us and that His forgiveness puts us under an obligation to forgive and thus to free ourselves, otherwise His forgiveness is an empty, hollow and frustrated thing.

Is love, the love of others, something we can earn? Probably not—we can earn respect but love isn't for sale. Like the love of God, we may only stand in wonder and hold it in trembling, mortal hands.

Sin is involved when we try too hard. We are not our own saviours. We are not permitted to take total responsibility for ourselves, either for our bloopers or our victories; nor can we allow ourselves to believe that our relationship with God is in escrow awaiting payment on our part before title passes.

Grace is the secret of freedom. To be saved by grace is to find both divine acceptance and self-acceptance in the love of God, a love which the life and death of Jesus confirms. Freed from the

172

illusion that we somehow can pay our way through life, we become the authentically free people of this earth, more understanding of the frailties of others, more human, and more qualified to live in the city of God.

When some of the new African nations first asserted independence from colonial rule, natives who lived their whole lives in the bush, and received only rumors about the new freedom they had been awarded, made their way to urban capitals with containers in which they hoped to carry some of the mystical stuff back to their tribal villages.

There is something both melancholy and thrilling about dusty men making their way into the capital with battered suitcases in order to claim their freedom. Perhaps a battered suitcase is better than nothing, better than the slavery that is not even recognized when men attempt to go it alone and know nothing of the word of grace.

Do you feel like a free person? Are you trying to make it under your own steam? Or have you discovered the secret of the gracious life? In a life which is exempt from the necessity of trying to prove or preserve itself, one is never too busy to laugh, too proud to cry, too self-centered to give thanks, or too blind to notice how generous God has been.

28

Our Church Approves of Gambling

How do I know that God is good? I don't
I gamble like a man
I bet my life
Upon one side in life's great war. I must
I can't stand out. I must take sides. The man
Who is a neutral in this fight is not
A man.

G. A. STUDDERT-KENNEDY

IN THE FOURTH GRADE I got a love letter from Myrtle Thompson, who was more advanced in her feelings than I. I was barely ten, and more interested in playing baseball, learning to play the harmonica and caddying on Saturday afternoons. When I got that long, impassioned love letter from Myrtle, I didn't know what to do with it. I took it home and showed it to my mother.

Since then, I have discovered that love is terribly important after all—the love of persons, the correct sort of love of yourself, love for God and truth and love for the world. Which all adds up to the love of life.

Love is full of risks. There is no possibility of loving without taking large chances, without becoming a showboat gambler. A love affair with life, if it is to be that and not an illicit weekend in a cheap motel, has to be put together out of the raw material of commitment. For Christians, the core of a committed life is a relationship with the God who has revealed Himself in Jesus Christ. Christians do not look upon life as simply a wheel of fortune. Neither are they unmindful that faith, by its very nature, is similar to a paratrooper's leap.

Ecclesiastes describes a man who tried in many ways to exploit his humanity, and in all of them he was successful; but he wound up saying, at the end of a long string of victories, "I hated life." He sought pleasure in things that were entertaining. He obtained an excellent education. He drank wine. He went into business and became rich. He married. He became interested in horticulture. He built a home. He traveled. He was elected to high office in Jerusalem. He had good health. He had it made; still he hated life!

This Old Testament book of wisdom represents a healthy realism. In some ways it seems more in touch than the New Testament. It pictures life as total vanity and men's efforts to deal with the world as inconsequential. It's a long way from Paul who calls men as "fellow workers for God." If we must choose, we take Paul. Still, during a time when we are substantially impressed with our technical skills and our eminence in creation, Ecclesiastes is a balancer. For a man with a low opinion of life, he continues to have an exalted view of God. We reverse the order. We are

174

low on God, but excited by the world, perishable though it is. The Book of Ecclesiastes has a marvelous prologue.

A generation goes, a generation comes, yet the earth stands firm forever. The sun rises, the sun sets; then to its place it speeds and there it rises. Southward goes the wind, then turns to the north; it turns and turns again; back then to its circling goes the wind. Into the sea all the rivers go, and yet the sea is never filled, and still to their goal the rivers go. All things are wearisome. No man can say that eyes have not had enough of seeing, ears their fill of hearing. What was will be again; what has been done will be done again; and there is nothing new under the sun. Take anything of which it may be said, 'Look now, this is new.' Already, long before our time, it existed. Only no memory remains of earlier times, just as in times to come next year itself will not be remembered.

THE JERUSALEM BIBLE

These are powerful arguments. But there is an alternative.

The love of life begins in the recognition that choice is involved. Life is not self-validating. While there are details about our life that lead us to believe that God is concerned, other evidence seems to add up to the conclusion that either God is a myth, or does not care or is helpless to do anything about the mess.

Job warns against trying to make gods of ourselves. It is not arrogant to say that if we decide to love this human situation of ours, we will need to bet the whole pile and refuse to let go.

There will be times for us when the world will look as if it has betrayed us. If we decide we love life because life has been good to us, we'd better think again. Faith is not a bargain. When we love, we are in danger of getting hurt. The ultimate tragedy is to be frightened into withdrawal by risks that keep us from loving at all. When people stand in the midst of dark and heavy sorrow, we can only hold them hard and say, "This is the way it has to be. If we love hard and deeply, then our sorrow will be like that, too. But it's worth it. It's just that one is the price of the other."

175

The love of life involves unilateral commitment. It must have this unconditional quality or it isn't love. It's cotton candy. God may not be so Almighty after all, but He is creatively working out historical possibilities as He goes along. Having appreciated that God is caught up in a game of Risk, too, we must take sides. We will not love life if we have no stake in its outcome.

Christians believe God cares about history and that He is involved with its outcome. This means life is moral and what a man does with his life, and what we do with the world's life is of infinite significance. We can't prove this. We can write it off as a foolish dream and call it a bankrupt idea. We can bet our money elsewhere or say, by faith, "The world matters, and I matter."

A hatred of life arises in people at both ends of the economic spectrum. Like Ecclesiastes, people who have too much are apt to be weary of life and cynical about it. People who have nothing and little hope of changing their condition also find life a drag and a burden. Jurgen N. Möltmann names these two forms of despair. One he calls a Promethean hopelessness, the hopelessness of the powerful—a man who is frustrated when he doesn't get everything he wants, or cannot make the rest of the world do as he wants.

The second is the hopelessness of Sisyphus, the hopelessness of resignation and defeat.

In between stands a man in love.

"Go. Sell everything you have and give it to the poor, and you will have treasure in heaven. Then, come, follow me." Jesus said something like that to a rich man. To another, ground under the heavy heel of adversity, He said that those who hunger are blessed now, for they will be satisfied. To all men went the invitation to take up their crosses daily and follow Him for He has come that their joy might be full.

This is on a different wave length from the man who says, "I tried Palm Beach and I tried Zen. I drank Scotch and I owned a Continental. But somehow, nothing seemed to matter very much." A love affair with life involves taking sides—and not just for the weekend!

This affair also flourishes in people who practice the art of thanksgiving. If we love life, then we are thankful. Is that it—or the other way around?

176

The Christian begins with thankfulness. Following Paul's counsel, he tries to give thanks in everything. He doesn't wait to see how life is coming out. He begins the day and ends it with gratitude. Even when things are falling apart, rather than cursing, he gives thanks that God is an unfailing supply of courage. When he quarrels with his lot, it is in the spirit of Robert Frost who once remarked that he had a lover's quarrel with the world. Urban man quarrels with the city because he cares what happens to it.

Into the void of doubt and the emptiness of unanswered questions, man has been trying to find something to relieve the hurt of his soul. He has often tried to make human love carry the burden of his need. He has tried to find in the human equation that which can be found, so the Christian believes, only in the ecstacy of a communion with God. Mathew Arnold lived a hundred years ago, but he speaks for contemporary man quite well:

> Ah, love, let us be true
> To one another! for the world, which seems
> To lie before us like a land of dreams,
> So various, so beautiful, so new
> Hath really neither joy, nor love, nor light
> Nor certitude, nor peace, nor help for pain.

Over and over these days we find sentences like these.

Love, the love between two people, has become a sort of substitute Christ, a redeemer through which men hope to gain salvation, cleansing and significance. It has become the last desperate resource of spirit against organization, of meaning within chaos; a protest, even a defiance, of the trivial and dishonorable world in which men are compelled to exist.

It's no good. We discover to our chagrin that this attitude toward love proposes that we should amuse one another to escape frustration. It suggests that we solve the problem of our acceptance and worth as human beings for each other, since we have no God to supply us with the dignity we crave.

Maturity comes when we move beyond the satisfaction of being loved to the larger satisfaction of loving. When we push beyond what Erich Fromm calls the prison cell of aloneness and feel the potency of producing love by loving, we outgrow the dependency on being loved.

To love—is it to flee or is it to find? Is this not one of the greatest issues of our existence? The love which is flight away from reality is a dead-end street. It ends in disillusionment. All love, whether it is the love of the married couple or the love of the parent for his child, must be an arterial street along which the lover advances toward a new appreciation of the love of God. Human love is a prerequisite to knowing divine love. Sexually disappointed people are usually those who are trying to emulate the emotions of loving but have nothing to communicate.

Life lovers also understand that love is a window, always a window, never a door. We see through it. "Love," wrote John Galsworthy in *The Man of Property* "is no hot-house flower, but a wild plant, born of a wet night, born of an hour of sunshine; sprung from wild seed, blown along the road by a wild wind. A wild plant that, when it blooms by chance within the hedge of our gardens, we call a flower; and when it blooms outside we call a weed; but, flower or weed, whose scent and colour are always wild!"

Hate and love are both four-letter words. Philosopher Schiller has defined hate as a prolonged form of suicide. He didn't add a parallel statement about love, but he could have. He could have said that love is an extended form of life. Hate is part of our emotional equipment, but it needs to be reserved for those things that deserve it. The church is called to be busy hating things which divide men and alienate them from one another. To hate lust and lies and cruelty and war and ignorance and fear is to let God make His appeal through us.

When we love, we are alive—when we love we see—when we really love and know love as its object, we are finished running and there is no need to hide. We're at life's destination and we can turn off the motor and look around. This is what life is for.

29

The Endless Summer
Evening: Zero Weather

And we have eyes no more for the dark pillars
                     or the freezing windows,
Ears for the rumorous cloister of the chimes
                     of time above our heads:
For we are sunken in the summer of our adoration,
And plunge, down, down into the fathoms of our
                            secret joy
That swims with indefinable fire.

And we will never see the copper sunset
Linger a moment, like an echo, on the frozen hill
Then suddenly die an hour before the Angelus.

For we have found our Christ, our August
Here in the zero days before Lent—

THOMAS MERTON

A YOUNG MAN, Bruce Brown, and some friends went around the world in search of the best surfing beaches. They arranged their itinerary in such a way that wherever they went and whenever they went, it was summer. They visited all five continents, and used thousands of feet of fantastic color film to record crashing water and daring feats on surfboards. This was later edited into a full-length movie, *The Endless Summer.*

When we've enjoyed a particular summer, we may very well have the feeling that we would like it to be endless. The great and greatest moments of life are ones we wish might never end. We'd like to capture such moments and save them—"carry moonbeams home in a jar." But time sweeps them away, and we go on to new experiences.

The endless summer might also suggest personal renewal—the kind of renewal which often happens to us during the summer months but which is no seasonal thing at all.

The Christian life is a life of constant renewal. It is a life of constant discovery. It is always unfolding, and always full of surprise. It is the life of endless summer.

> New every morning is the love
> Our wakening and uprising prove;
> Through sleep and darkness safely brought,
> Restored to life and power and thought.
>
> New mercies, each returning day,
> Hover around us while we pray;
> New perils past, new sins forgiven,
> New thoughts of God, new hopes of heaven.
>
> JOHN KEBLE

Each morning's awakening from sleep is a return from death, a repeat of resurrection.

If we're in the ice-cream or air-conditioning business, summer may be our toughest season. But for most it is a time to let up, to unbend, to catch our breath, to get out into the surf and let it knock us down, to play and through long evenings, to ponder, to review and to evaluate our direction.

Could this represent the tunnel vision of the secure, the middle class, the reasonably affluent one who isn't fighting for his survival?

Peter Schrag in a *Saturday Review* article suggested, "It would be instructive for those with some vacation time to spend part of it, not in the Poconos or the Sierras, but in Appalachia in the places called Stinking Creek or Horse Creek—not in the customary watering places, but in front of an open hydrant in Bedford-

Stuyvesant—not on the fairways at the club, but in the tomato fields of South Jersey, where migrants are picking the crop."

Mr. Schrag asks, "Who really wants to see America? See America in Harlem or in Hough; see America in Lowndes County, Alabama. See America in public mental hospitals where one or two psychiatrists are supposed to care for two thousand patients. See America in the lines at the welfare offices and the induction centers. See America in dimly lit bus terminals at midnight, or in the lobbies of cheap hotels, or in the police precinct station houses of any city at two in the morning. This is the America of Lee Harvey Oswald, James Earl Ray and Sirhan Sirhan, a world of grimy walk-ups and blasted hopes, of cigarette burns and disinfectant, of bare light bulbs and cheap hamburgers."

"Do not be conformed to the world," wrote Paul, "but be transformed by the renewal of your mind" (Romans 12:2 RSV).

Look at conformity first. Conformity is both desirable and dangerous. Some is the basis of civilization, law, art and freedom. John MacKay, athletic coach at the University of Southern California, says it takes a large helping of it to build a championship football team. Dissonance is musical nonconformity, but it contains the possibilities of beauty because it stands in contrast to order, harmony and conforming tones.

Today we witness a great deal of nonconformity—bizarre dress, flaunting of standards and dropping out. Some is pathetic; some is part of a message the straight world needs to hear. Nonconformist youths are most important, not for their numbers or their excesses, but for their eloquent questions. Conformity makes the gears shift smoothly, but perhaps at a high price. In the Army conformity is a way of life, but who wants life run like a battalion? Total conformity is dictatorship. Total absence of conformity is chaos. The story of America is the story of an attempt to walk a creative middle way. This is why the National Democratic Convention in Chicago was so important, for this was the issue written large—the Achilles' heel of our total society was exposed.

One style of conformity which needs to be watched and resisted is the conformity of habit. A poem called "The Calf Path" tells about a calf who took a winding path through a pasture. The calf nibbled here and there, moving aimlessly along. He was fol-

181

lowed by another calf who ate and sniffed his way along the same twisting route. Later, a farmer in search of his wandering livestock took the same path looking for them. As the poem progresses the path becomes a marked trail, then a village street, and finally a busy boulevard. But it stays as crooked as it was the day the first innocent little calf meandered through the field.

Much conformity is the result of fear, the fear of being challenged, noticed, criticized or punished. Thank God for those who break this barrier, and for those who still follow the light of conscience and take their stands regardless of consequences.

Some is moral laziness. W. H. Auden's "Unknown Citizen," just rolled along with the tide. "When there was peace, he was for peace; when there was war, he went"—the perfect outer-directed man.

Other conformity is the result of being tired. We simply can't fight any longer. Some is the by-product of being too secure. If you hold four aces, you're not going to ask for a new deal.

What Paul is telling us is that the Christian life modeled on Jesus is always life in conflict. It is forever uncomfortable; it is always troubled by a vision of something greater, something better which will not allow it to rest, to conform, or to drift with the wind.

Eternal dissatisfaction is a gift.

> When God at first made man,
> Having a glass of blessings standing by;
> Let us (said He) pour on him all we can:
> Let the world's riches, which dispersèd lie,
>   Contract into a span.
>
> So strength first made a way;
> Then beauty flowed, then wisdom, honour, pleasure:
> When almost all was out, God made a stay,
> Perceiving that alone of all His treasure
>   Rest in the bottom lay.
>
> For if I should (said He)
> Bestow this jewel also on My creature,

182

He would adore My gifts instead of Me,
And rest in Nature, not the God of Nature,
   So both should losers be.

Yet let him keep the rest,
But keep them with repining restlessness:
Let him be rich and weary, that at least,
If goodness lead him not, yet weariness
   May toss him to My breast.

GEORGE HERBERT

The New Testament says we are co-creators with God, called to mold the world according to the will of Christ. It says: don't run from the world, don't hide from it and don't despise it. Take it into your arms but don't let it mold you. You mold it on behalf of Him.

". . . But be transformed by the renewal of your mind." To be transformed is to be changed. That's the literal meaning of the word, to be steadily, dynamically changed into something more than we are.

Not all change is progress, but there is little progress without it. Life is moving. The Spirit is busy. The creative activity of God is as authentic now as it was when the mountains were exploding and the routes of the stars being settled.

We renew our minds by allowing them to change. We renew them by exposure to new and painful ideas, new experiences and new feelings. And we renew them by involvement. As long as we remain distant observers we do not allow ourselves to be tested and we stay where we are. When we do get involved in the life of the church, in politics, in urban problems, in the issues of this fragile drama, we will be renewed. We may get bruised, but we will not rot.

Once in the course of a vacation trip, our family stopped briefly at Eureka, Nevada, on our way from Ghost Ranch to Lake Tahoe. It is a ghost town now. It stands there all alone in the desert, and it was shivery cold when we stopped there for gas and something to eat. We settled for a bowl of hot vegetable soup at one of the town's two dingy restaurants. A small printed folder, which came with our change, told of a time when thousands of frontiersmen lived in Eureka, mining the lead, drinking whisky, and battling their way west.

Today the church lives its life on a dozen new edges—the frontiers of radical theology, world involvement, ecumenicity, and the emergence of a theologically sophisticated laity. The church has a conservative image, but she is learning to take bold chances and to become a pioneer again.

Some of us have been around quite awhile. Perhaps the earth begins to seem a bit old, but it needn't. The earth is still adolescently, excitingly young. Our minds are young, too, if we hold them up daily as an offering and ask God to dust them off for us.

Recently we got out some brass candlesticks and polished them. We had forgotten how beautiful they were. We set them near the fireplace where they added new charm to the living room; then we invited our passing neighbors in to look at them.

Self-renewal is like that. We begin cleaning out debris, wiping off old dust and stain; then we become exhibits of the authentically awakened life. "A city set on a hill cannot be hid" (Matthew 5:14 RSV). Grab your surfboard and let's get going!

30
Today Is the First Day of the Rest of Your Life

Look to this day!
For it is life, the very life of life.
In its brief course lie all the verities and realities
    of your existence:
The bliss of growth,
The glory of action,
The splendor of beauty.

184

For yesterday is but a dream,
And tomorrow is only a vision;
But today well-lived makes every yesterday a dream
    of happiness,
And every tomorrow a vision of hope.
Look well therefore to this day!

Translated from SANSKRIT

LOS ANGELES is a terrible place to visit but you probably would enjoy living here, especially if getting home from the office meant a regular late-afternoon drive along Sunset Boulevard toward the sea. As the twisting thoroughfare winds westward past Beverly Hills and UCLA, through the center of the old Will Rogers ranch with its sycamores and palisades, it leads toward a rare psychedelic splendor as the sun says good-bye on its way to the Islands.

Sunrise requires no locale. It is bells and bugles wherever we behold the arrival of that golden wafer upon which existence depends. For those who are lonely, recently wounded, trying to comprehend they've but a short time to live, without work, or harboring a secret they must either keep or face public crucifixion the light comes cruelly. On most days, and for most men, sunrise is God's new offer, and the chance to start over, to try again.

The Christian faith, by its emphasis on forgiveness and resurrection, has always been identified with the morning and with what lies ahead. At the same time, it is a rearview mirror, examining what God has already done. Much of its message is proclaimed as retrospect. If the Christian man is a watchman, waiting for daybreak, he also is a man of memories, pondering the road behind.

It is the present which has power to excite us most, for it is then we can do most. The past has the power to tyrannize us by nostalgia. The future, that glamour fuel which keeps our engines firing and our alarm clocks ringing, can become a tyranny of dreams. The razor's edge between the two, upon which we dance the dance of life, is Now.

Biblical man believed one should help one another to stand firm in the faith every day while it is still called today. A. M. Sullivan put it another way: "There are two majorities, son, though you ask me no question. The nameless dead, the unborn legions of time, but we are the thin minority, the living, who hold God's sceptre of light."

The past can refer to a most honorable ancestor, a wedding day, a prison record, or a preoccupation with right-wing politics. It is both a benediction and a problem. Youth born since the Depression and World War II are bored stiff by continuous reference to those events. Today there are new sufferings to be suffered, new battlegrounds on which to die.

While there is nothing in the Decalogue about refusing to accept your own times it is still some sort of sin to complain, "Lord, I don't want to be me; I want to be someone else. You put me in the wrong generation."

A bluegrass muse meditating upon the splendor of yesterday wrote:

What curious keys unlock the different room where our treasures are kept. I recently stumbled onto a postcard written to me by my mother seven years ago. It helped me remember who I am. A snatch of song, the pungent smell of an earthen cellar, a distant whistle in the night, the soft look of a rain swept street. There is a little click of the lock and suddenly we find ourselves remembering something we had almost forgotten we ever knew. Then the past is no longer the past. Part of it lives again. It comes to illumine and interpret the present and tell us who we are. If only I could command the sun to stop where it was in the sky and hold all the white mists where they were in the air. If I could keep the pasture daisies as white and the wild roses as pink as they were now. If I could keep the sawbriers in clusters with their red-tinted leaves. If I could make this pasture and time stand still, I'd do it!

JESSE STUART

The past also has the power to redeem. The conservative is no fool. Though accused of being too concerned with the past and

186

inclined to steer by his rearview mirror, he appreciates the wisdom of using the cumulative experience of thousands of years in appraising the meaning of the next twenty minutes.

A Christian stands between memory and hope. Richard Cardinal Cushing wrote a Christmas letter for all children in which he said, "To be able to remember the gift of love in one's childhood is the greatest gift any man shall have received in his life—because from the gift of love and the good memory of love, a man can become the whole person he was meant to be in the sight of God."

Faith also has a keen interest in the future and has its own portraits of it. These become tyrannical, too, if they divert us from an authentic acceptance of the present world with its imperfections and disappointments and reduce our confidence in God to mere longing.

The liberal is criticized because he is too attentive to the future, but he is not stupid and understands that new occasions teach new duties. Ours is a world in fantastic motion and its issues cannot be uncritically settled by precedent. Each night as we lie down to sleep, God takes a piece of the future and lays it on our doorstep. He means us to claim and be excited by that gift.

Sunrise is transition from yesterday to today, and the two days are the tall gates of a great city just beginning to swing open to our sight. Some words from the preface of *Los Angeles* by Paul C. Johnson partly explain why its fun to live here.

A city of ceaseless change and innovation, impatient of precedent, inhabited by people who do things on a grand scale, solving problems with flair and imagination, creating a man-made landscape of surprises and contrasts, tending the sophisticated needs of far-out technology.

Now is the moment that rushes beneath our feet like railroad ties beneath a fast train. "Help one another to stand firm in the faith every day, while it is still called 'today'" (Hebrews 3:13 PHILLIPS). Those words mean worship God today while it is in your power to do so. Get rid of your hates, your grudges and greeds—

don't wait. Live today. Rejoice today. Drink of the world as it is, not withholding your interest and affection until it changes for the better.

Rearview mirrors, sunrises, now—for men in every city, each represents a facet of the grace of God. From out of faith's past we learn that ". . . not in utter nakedness, but trailing clouds of glory do we come from God." In faith's future, we find an antidote to fear and the confidence that there is so much yet to be. In faith's present, we can find a meaning for today, a work to do, a song to sing, a duty to perform and a life to live. Today is the first day of the rest of our lines together. Let's put our arms around the city of man and be deliciously glad.